"I have been around Conservative politics a [...]
to-back majority governments with a divers[...]
senting all parts of the country. We made tough decisions grounded in evidence-based
public policy on the economy, the environment, human rights, and the implementation
of the GST. We made Canada competitive and set up the opportunity to balance the
budget. Right now, our country needs a strong Conservative leader who can rebuild such
a coalition and take Tasha Kheiriddin's astute analysis of new voter trends to reach those
constituencies to win the next general election."

— **BRIAN MULRONEY,** *eighteenth prime minister of Canada*

"Starting with a frank, honest, and articulate review of where Canadian conservatism is
today and how it got there, Tasha Kheiriddin quickly pivots and outlines a compelling
opportunity for the future built on a foundation of hope, growth, and opportunity. This
is a refreshing and uplifting work from a leading conservative thinker and down-in-the-
trenches activist who sees the bigger picture and knows what it takes to get things done."

— **RICK PETERSON,** *founder of Peterson Capital and leadership candidate
for the Conservative Party of Canada*

"In this era of political division—between the Left and the Right, between the woke and
the 'deplorables'—long-time Conservative Party activist Tasha Kheiriddin courageously
wades into the fray, offering a common-sense solution for the future political success of
a revitalized Conservative Party of Canada. For those looking for a political home, this
is a must-read."

— **JANET ECKER,** *former member of the Ontario legislature and Minster of
Finance, Harris Government*

"A very astute observation of the evolution of the conservative cause in Canada by an
ardent, committed Conservative."

— **GERRY ST. GERMAIN,** *former Minister of Transport and Minister of
Forests, Mulroney Government Senator*

"Tasha Kheiriddin has been involved in the conservative movement for over thirty years.
Her unique perspective on what it will take to win over cities and towns that were once
bedrocks for Conservatives is a must-read for every Conservative activist and anyone
who cares about Canada having a strong democracy."

— **WALIED SOLIMAN,** *Chair, Norton Rose Fulbright Canada LLP*

"*The Right Path* is a compelling read, carefully constructed by Tasha Kheiriddin. Her
ability to analyze the political landscape and story-tell is unique. She asks the existential
question: What is conservatism? By the end of the book, you'll have the answer—and it
may be different than you expected. If you're a politico, this is a must-read."

— **VONNY SWEETLAND,** *writer and radio host*

THE
RIGHT
PATH

*How Conservatives Can
Unite, Inspire and Take
Canada Forward*

TASHA KHEIRIDDIN

FOREWORD BY LISA MacCORMACK RAITT

The Right Path: How Conservatives Can Unite, Inspire, and Take Canada Forward
© Ottawa, 2022, Optimum Publishing International and Tasha Kheiriddin

First Edition Published by Optimum Publishing International, a division of JF Moore
Lithographers Inc. All rights reserved. No part of this publication may be reproduced in any
form or by any means whatsoever or stored in a data base without permission in writing from
the publisher, except by a reviewer who may quote passages of customary brevity in review.

LIBRARY AND ARCHIVES CANADA CATALOGUING IN PUBLICATION

Tasha Kheiriddin, 1970
The Right Path, How conservatives can unite, inspire and take Canada forward. I. Title

ISBN 978-0-88890-331-0 (Paperback)
ISBN 978-0-88890-332-7 (ePub)

Printed and bound in Canada

For information on rights or any submissions, please write to Optimum:

Optimum Publishing International
144 Rochester Avenue
Toronto, Ontario
M4N 1P1
Dean Baxendale, President
www.optimumpublishinginternational.com
Twitter @opibooks

For Papa, who always told me, "Take the middle way."

CONTENTS

FOREWORD

Lisa MacCormack Raitt

The Conservative Party of Canada has always been referred to as the "Big Tent" party: a gathering of people who share the same values of smaller government, lower taxes, and greater freedom while maintaining self-identified characteristics. I was raised Catholic on Canada's East Coast, studied law in Ontario, and stayed there to raise my family in the suburbs around Toronto. I am pro-choice, socially liberal, and worry greatly about environmentally sustainable long-term economic growth. My closest friend in the party was raised Mennonite in the Prairies, is pro-life, socially conservative, and worries about oil and gas workers being displaced in the move to a "Just Transition." We both passionately support our party and each other.

As I look to the United States, I often wonder if my best friend and I would find ourselves diverging in the polarization so apparent in American society. On paper, she and I would seem to line up in opposing camps, but here in Canada we have a home where we can find more similarities than differences, and over the past fifteen years, we have remained close friends. I have often assured myself that we are different here in Canada and that polarization will not take hold here.

In *The Right Path*, Tasha Kheiriddin lays out why polarization should be a concern for Canadians. Tasha has been a strong voice for conservative policies in Canada for decades and critically analyzes what is happening in Canada now, why it is happening, and provides some thoughts on how to move forward. The backdrop to this analysis is a very current leadership race in the Conservative Party of Canada, which she uses effectively to show the turning point that we are approaching.

The events of the past twelve months are impossible to ignore, as are the impacts on my party. I haven't always agreed with my fellow Conservatives on issues. As an MP, I marched in a pride parade, and as a minister of the Crown, I voted in favour of an NDP private members' bill on trans rights. Yet, I have always felt welcome, and that my opinion (while not always agreed with) was valued. I wonder today if I would be afforded the same luxury.

During the 2016–2017 leadership campaign that I took part in, "Liberal Lite" was often whispered behind my back by the pro–Maxime Bernier members. I shrugged it off as new members being brought into the party not fully understanding that we are a big tent. In this leadership campaign and the previous one, I saw sitting MPs on opposing campaigns accusing each other of being "liberals" with derision. As Tasha points out, there seems to be a desire to put people through a purity test—as though some Conservatives are more legitimate than others. If you aren't of a certain shade of blue you are not only not welcome—you are wrong and ridiculed. It's one thing for those of us under the Big Blue Tent to natter about our own to each other—it is quite a different thing for us to step outside the tent and declare others to not be true-enough Conservatives.

As Tasha points out, with this kind of name-calling, one does have to wonder what makes a Conservative, and she expertly brings us through the historical context of how the party has changed over the years, including its most recent changes. She clearly explains that understanding who we are will be essential to the one goal that binds all Conservative Party members—replacing the Liberal–NDP coalition-by-contract government with a strong, stable Conservative-majority federal government.

This book is not a book that sets out to provide a list of complaints without a plan for moving forward. Tasha takes the time to consider what the paths to victory for the Conservative Party may look like. These are worthy of consideration by any leader of the party. Choosing which path will be the purview of the next leader, but campaigns matter, and the next

Conservative leader's success may be aided by a formidable advantage.

If reports are true, the Conservative Party of Canada now has over six hundred thousand members. On average, this is about one thousand eight hundred members per riding, though membership sales aren't uniform across the 338 ridings. Even if this translates to somewhere between five hundred and a thousand motivated members who volunteer for the 2025 campaign in a given riding, that sheer amount of people on the ground would make for a very strong campaign for each and every Conservative candidate. As my former campaign manager pointed out—with that many volunteers available, the Conservative Party could form the next government.

What remains to be seen is which message will win the day—will the Big Blue Tent hold, or will we dissolve into populism? I do hope that the coalition finds itself intact, not only for the Conservative Party's electoral future but also for those individual members who may not seem politically similar, yet can find each other in an inclusive party that makes space for them to discover they are similar enough to be best friends.

THE DAY TRUMP CAME TO CANADA

On January 29, 2022, Donald Trump came to Canada. Not literally, of course; on that day he was actually at a rally in Conroe, Texas, three thousand kilometres away. But his spirit, and his words, floated up over the border and found their first tangible foothold in the politics of our nation.

"We want those great Canadian truckers to know that we are with them all the way . . . [They are] doing more to defend American freedom than our own leaders by far."[1]

Those truckers weren't just big rig drivers protesting the bilateral vaccine mandate that prevented unvaccinated drivers from crossing the Canada–US border. They included thousands of other people— people who had lost their businesses, whose kids had missed months of school, or who were just fed up and felt they "had to do something." They converged on Ottawa to demand the lifting of a host of pandemic restrictions: vaccine mandates, mask mandates, business and school closures. The most common refrain was, "We want our lives back."

Who did they blame for this situation? That was clear. After calls for "freedom," the most ubiquitous words on their lips and on their signs were "Fuck Trudeau," in reference to Canada's twenty-third prime minister. Never mind that 90 percent of the rules they objected to fell under provincial jurisdiction. Justin Trudeau hadn't shuttered their stores, kept their kids at home, or imposed curfews, but he was their lightning rod, their woker-than-thou symbol of everything that has gone wrong in this country over the past few years.

If you'd gone looking for the PM while they were descending on the city, you wouldn't have found him; due to security threats, he and his family had been moved to a safe location. In addition, one of his children had tested positive for COVID-19 (Trudeau later tested positive himself). Still, his opponents gleefully accused him of hiding. Unlike his father, Pierre, who as prime minister smiled while he was pelted with rocks and bottles at a Saint-Jean-Baptiste Day parade in 1969,[2] Justin didn't appear to like it when people didn't, er, like *him*. In fact, ever since his government was reduced to a minority, governing had apparently become so unpleasant that he delegated much of the task to his deputy prime minister and minister of finance, Chrystia Freeland.

On January 31, Trudeau issued a terse statement to reporters from his cottage at Harrington Lake. "Over the past few days, Canadians were shocked, and frankly, disgusted by the behaviour displayed by some people protesting in our nation's capital. We are not intimidated by those who hurl insults and abuse small-business workers and steal food from the homeless. We won't give in to those who fly racist flags. We won't cave to those who engage in vandalism or dishonour the memory of our veterans."[3]

The events Trudeau referred to made headlines for days. There were multiple reports of protesters berating and harassing hotel staff for requiring protesters to wear masks on the premises, which they refused to do.[4] Anti-maskers also swarmed the Rideau Centre, Ottawa's main downtown shopping mall, prompting the landlords to shut it down. Protesters intimidated staff at a nearby soup kitchen, Shepherds of Good Hope, and took food meant for the homeless.[5] They draped the Terry Fox statue on Parliament Hill in an upside-down Canadian flag and a sign reading "Mandate Freedom." They urinated on the National War Memorial. They honked truck horns at all hours of the day and night. Making the rounds on social media were images of pickups adorned with Confederate flags, the maple leaf defaced with swastikas, and Donald Trump 2024 banners. Ottawa felt like a city under siege. Law and order, it would appear, had left the building.

Where were the Conservatives in all this? Unlike Trudeau, several Tory politicians eagerly waded into the fray. Pierre Poilievre, Leslyn Lewis, and Andrew Scheer high-fived protesters and posted supportive clips to social media. Leader Erin O'Toole tweeted snaps of himself talking to truckers. Some Conservatives were downright jubilant. Rachel Curran, the public policy manager for Canada at Facebook and the former policy director for Prime Minister Stephen Harper, tweeted, "Agree, it's got a real Canada Day celebratory vibe despite the bitter cold. Hopefully more music and flag-waving and partying tomorrow."

Maybe not. Curran's Twitter account was subsequently deactivated, perhaps because her employer felt that a "celebratory vibe" shouldn't include hate symbols like the Viking helmets on Soldiers of Odin jackets. O'Toole later called out the bad actors, including those who had desecrated the statue of Terry Fox and the Tomb of the Unknown Soldier.[6] Another MP, Michael Cooper, condemned the presence of Nazi symbols that were visible in the background while he was giving a television interview with CBC TV.

But this backpedalling was largely seen as too little, too late. For many Canadians, images of screaming anti-maskers and Canadian flags adorned with swastikas became the defining visuals of the event. And Conservatives were seen to be supporting it, standing with the people who were there.

The protests would prove to be a watershed for the Conservative Party. Within less than a week, caucus turfed O'Toole as leader, in a vote of seventy-six to thirty-four. Within days of this coup, Poilievre announced his run for leader and, in a stellar example of data mining, started a petition for Canadians to "reclaim control of their lives" (and to potentially sign up thousands of members).[7] When asked on January 31 by House leader Mark Holland to join the government in asking the protesters to go home, Poilievre shot back that "the problem is [that the government has] shown no respect for the people . . . the honest, hard-working, shirt-off-your-back-type people that this prime minister keeps attacking."[8]

After the initial weekend, however, it appeared that a lot of those hard-working people had left town. In their wake, fringe elements moved in, including Romana Didulo, a conspiracy theorist and the self-styled true "Queen of Canada." Protesters set up bouncy castles, barbeques, and hot tubs and proceeded to host nightly street parties. Convoy organizer Pat King led karaoke nights on an unlicensed outdoor sound stage—this in a city where, just six years prior, two kids were fined for setting up a lemonade stand without a permit.[9] (King would later be charged with perjury, intimidation, obstructing police, counselling to commit intimidation, counselling to commit mischief, counselling to obstruct police, and disobeying a court order.)[10] One of the iconic images of the events was a short video of a protester named Ryan, clad in nothing but a bathing suit, jaws grinding in an apparent meth-induced frenzy, bellowing "Fuck Justin Trudeau! Freedooom!" complete with appropriate hand gestures, in minus-eighteen-degree-Celsius weather.

But there was also a far more sinister side to the gathering. In a post-mortem a month later, National Security and Intelligence Advisor Jody Thomas concluded, "The people who organized that protest, and there were several factions there, there's no doubt (they) came to overthrow the government."[11] Some of the organizers, including King, had openly expressed white supremacist views.[12] Some protesters had called for this to be Canada's January 6, in reference to the riot at the US Capitol a year earlier. They went so far as to set up a "command centre" ringed with trucks in Major's Hill Park at the base of Parliament Hill.

The protests also spread far beyond the city of Ottawa, popping up at border crossings in British Columbia, Alberta, and Ontario. At the Ambassador Bridge, which connects Windsor to Detroit, protests shut down traffic for a week and caused an estimated $3 to $6 billion in losses due to stalled trade.[13] The city of Windsor said that responding to the situation with law enforcement and other personnel cost close to $6 million, for which it requested reimbursement from the provincial and federal governments.[14] At the protest in Coutts, Alberta, police seized long guns, handguns, body armour, and large amounts of ammunition and high-capacity magazines. Eleven individuals faced charges ranging from weapons and mischief to conspiracy to murder.[15] And in British Columbia, protesters at the Pacific Highway Border Crossing attacked a number of journalists—spitting, striking, and harassing them—prompting the police to intervene.[16]

Two weeks after the protests began, Poilievre told reporters on Parliament Hill, "Yes to peaceful protests. No to blockades." Fair enough, but what would he do to end them? "It's real simple. Listen to the science. Do what the other provinces and the other countries are doing: end the mandates and the restrictions so the protesters can get back to their lives and their jobs."[17]

In other words, give in to the protesters' demands. For some Conservatives watching at home, it seemed as though the CPC had been turned on its head. Where was the party of law and order that under Prime Minister Stephen Harper brought in mandatory minimum sentences and demanded increased accountability for criminal acts? Where was the party that had demanded the government put an end to blockades by hereditary chiefs of the Wet'suwet'en First Nation and their supporters two years previously? And what had happened to the basic balance between rights and responsibilities extolled by the party's own constitution?

Answer: it had been drowned out in the cry of a single word, "Freedom." For the Conservatives supporting the protests, freedom took precedence over all other values and principles. But what did freedom mean anymore? For many of the assembled, it meant the freedom to do whatever they pleased: honk their horns at all hours of the day and night, park fifty-foot trucks wherever they chose, and disrupt the lives of an entire city full of people.

Freedom appeared to mean anarchy. Not exactly what the British granddaddy of conservatism, the philosopher Edmund Burke, had in mind in 1790 when he penned *Reflections on the Revolution in France*, decrying the Terror of the Jacobins and the chaos in the streets. Not exactly what Progressive Conservative prime minister John Diefenbaker thought of when he drafted the Canadian Bill of Rights in 1959 to guarantee equality before the law and protection of the law. And certainly not what Stephen Harper's Conservatives stood for when they were in power from 2006 to 2015.

How did Canadians feel about the convoy? An Ipsos poll

taken on February 8 and 9, after just over a week of protests, found some important fault lines. Forty-six percent of Canadians said they "may not agree with everything the people who have taken part in the truck protests in Ottawa have said, but their frustration is legitimate and worthy of our sympathy." Regionally, respondents in Alberta, Saskatchewan, and Manitoba, at 58 percent, were most likely to support this statement. Generationally, the eighteen to thirty-four-year-olds were the most likely to sympathize with those participating in the convoy, at 61 percent of respondents. Politically, most Conservative voters (59 percent) sided with this argument, with only half that percentage of Liberal voters agreeing. Bloc and NDP voters found themselves in the middle of that spectrum of support for the truckers, at 44 and 43 percent respectively.

Conversely, 54 percent of respondents believed that "what the people taking part in the truck protests in Ottawa have said and done is wrong and does not deserve any of our sympathy." Support for this proposition was highest among respondents aged fifty-five or older, followed by those aged thirty-five to fifty-four. Regionally, British Columbians most strongly denounced the trucker convoy (63 percent). Politically, 70 percent of Liberals opposed the convoy, while fewer NDP (57 percent), Bloc (56 percent), and Conservative voters (41 percent) held this position.

Six in ten respondents agreed that "the truck protest is mostly a group of anti-vaxxers and bigots intent on causing mayhem and they should not be allowed to protest." Oddly enough, at the same time, 37 percent of respondents reported that while they may not say it publicly, they agreed with a lot of what the protesters were fighting for. This rose to 63 percent of Conservative voters and 45 percent of Canadians aged eighteen to thirty-four. One in four said that they would have considered joining the truck protest if a small fringe group had not raised Nazi flags and shown their intolerance and racism. Thirty-eight percent of Conservative voters and 39 percent of those aged eighteen to thirty-four felt this way as well.[18]

The protests revealed Canada to be a house divided by age, geography, and political persuasion. The "Freedom Convoy" didn't just represent unvaccinated truckers affected by vaccine mandates. It represented

Westerners whose oil industry had been demonized for decades by environmentalists and more recently, by their own prime minister. It represented people disenfranchised by economic shifts from manufacturing economies to knowledge-based economies. It represented the effects of two years of pandemic restrictions, which shuttered a host of businesses and prevented young people from spreading their wings. It produced a large number of people who wanted relief from their despair, wanted to be heard, and most importantly, wanted to reclaim the status they had lost. And the truckers' protest spoke to them.

These "Convoy Conservatives" felt they were not sharing in the wealth of the rest of the country. They felt that despite doing the "right things"—working, saving, building a life for their families—they could not get ahead, and in many cases, were falling behind. They felt excluded and looked down on by "elites" who disrespected their choice of industry, employment, or vaccination status.

And in many respects, they were right. Earlier this year, I spoke to hundreds of Conservatives from across the country while contemplating a run for the Tory leadership, as well as dozens more in writing this book. Several conversations stood out. One was an Edmonton man, who will remain anonymous; I'll call him Frank. Frank complained bitterly about the state of affairs in Alberta. At sixty-eight, having worked all his life, this man has a house worth less today than it was four years ago. "Meanwhile, my friends in Toronto have seen their property values soar," Frank sighed. He was angry at the domination of Eastern elites who took from the West, but gave nothing back.

Then there was Vincent, a twenty-six year old francophone entrepreneur from the South Shore of Montreal. During the convoy, he drove up to Ottawa for two weekends and demonstrated with his girlfriend and cousin. "It was great to see people coming together, I hadn't seen people that happy for the past two years. I think people were just fed up." Vincent was not vaccinated: "It was my only way to express my disagreement with the government. If I got vaccinated, they would have counted me as agreeing with them." He had also never been a member of a political party before—but has since joined the Conservatives to support Poilievre.

A lot of Canadians are angry at the government, at the elites, and at the pandemic itself. One solution is to embrace the politics of anger. Like the trucker protest, anger is empowering. Convoy supporters want someone to listen. They want things to change. And they want someone to pay.

But Conservatives are divided as well. Not by traditional lines, such as fiscal conservatism, social conservatism, or libertarianism, but by something else: class. The new divide is between the "people" and the "elites." Problem is, those elites do not just dwell on the left, or within the Liberal establishment. They inhabit the Conservative Party as well.

At the opposite end of the spectrum from the Convoy Conservatives, you will find the "Club Conservatives." They are, as the name would suggest, the class of Conservatives who belong to the Albany Club in Toronto, or are part of the "Quebec Inc." crowd in Montreal. They are largely in the professions, like law or and finance; they are CEOs, communications experts, tech workers, and business owners. They are the "laptop class" who got to work from home during the pandemic, and who in many cases are better off than they were two years ago. And in the leadership race, they have been targeted just as much as the Liberals have.

Convoy Conservatives decry Club Conservatives as members of the Laurentian Elite, the class of "old-stock," Eastern Canada–based, liberal-minded Canadians that have long dominated Canadian academics, business, media, and politics. "Laurentian Elite" is a tag previously deployed against Trudeau and members of the Liberal Party, but it's now being used against other candidates in the leadership race. The chief target is former Quebec premier and federal Progressive Conservative (PC) leader Jean Charest. For his Convoy critics, Charest's sin is not simply that he led the Quebec Liberals for over a decade (in a province where, one should note, there was no provincial Conservative party, and the provincial Liberal party was a centre-right organization), but that he is a politician from Eastern Canada, a.k.a. the Establishment. In the us-versus-them world of class politics, this is automatically suspect. For Convoy Conservatives, Charest's PC past—as a minister in the government of Brian Mulroney, as party leader who held the party together when it fell to two seats, as Captain Canada in the 1995 referendum—doesn't count. They also ignore his fiscally conservative record while Quebec premier (Charest lowered taxes and left a surplus of $8 billion to his successor, CAQ leader François Legault), because it does not fit their "Liberal" narrative.

The champion of the Convoy Conservatives in the leadership race is Pierre Poilievre. Born in Alberta, Poilievre has represented the Ottawa-area riding of Nepean–Carleton for eighteen of his forty-two years. Known as a "take no prisoners"–style politician, he had built up a significant fan following prior to the leadership race based on his unrelenting attacks on Trudeau and his willingness to "tell it like it is." Poilievre is now putting as just much energy into demonizing elites—the "gatekeepers," as he calls them—in his populist bid to win the leadership. By the numbers, this plan appears to be working: Poilievre's camp claims to have signed up an astounding 311,958 members, more than the total signed up by all candidates in the 2019 leadership contest.[19]

But this us-versus-them strategy is also driving a stake in the heart of the Conservative family by pitting one set of Conservatives against another. This is not only causing dissent within, but sending a clear message to people watching from the outside, including "political orphans" like Red Tories and Blue Liberals. The message isn't just that Convoy Conservatives think Club Conservatives don't belong in their party, but that those political orphans don't either.

This new division along class lines is more difficult to navigate for the Conservative Party than its previous fault lines, because it is one that cannot readily be repaired by compromise. Previously, social conservatives, fiscal conservatives, Red Tories, and libertarians all had to put a little water in their wine, recognizing that without each other, they could not gain power, and thus would not achieve anything at all. Mulroney's and Harper's coalitions all involved compromise on issues such as abortion, the Constitution, and the size of government. But class is a different animal, because it pits elements of the party against each other on the very issue that previously bound them together: freedom.

No matter their crew, Conservatives could traditionally come together around issues of freedom, such as smaller government, less regulation, and freedom of speech. The word *freedom* has a storied history in conservative politics around the world. Republican president Ronald Reagan fought for freedom from communism. Conservative British prime minister Margaret Thatcher fought for freedom from overweening government. Here at home, Prime Minister Brian Mulroney championed free trade. Freedom had a noble ring to it, and represented the antithesis of autocracy.

But when freedom becomes equated with out-of-control street protests, hooliganism, and anti-social behaviour, it loses its lustre. Worse yet, in the toxic soup of US politics, freedom has become something else entirely. As *Globe and Mail* columnist Gary Mason noted, "For many, it's a word that has become code for white-identity politics and the Far Right's weapon of choice in the culture wars."[20] In the US House of Representatives, the most conservative members came together in a Freedom Caucus that now includes controversial Trump supporters like Marjorie Taylor Greene, Lauren Boebert, and Paul Gosar.[21] Greene is a conspiracy theorist who regularly talks with Trump, while Boebert equated Ukraine's nuclear demilitarization with US gun control.[22] Both women infamously heckled Biden during his State of the Union Address when he was talking about his deceased son, Beau. Not exactly the classiest display of "freedom" of speech.

Freedom is now tarnished. It is no longer a word that unites but one that divides. It has become about us versus them. The people versus the elites. And that is a major problem. For apart from these two groups, there is a large swath of the electorate who identify as neither Convoy nor Club, and sometimes, but not always, as Conservative. They are what we'll call "Common Sense" Canadians, the kind of pragmatic middle-class voters who have been the backbone of electoral victory for both Tories and Liberals for the past century. They include small-business owners, soccer moms, and middle-class suburban families. Increasingly, they are first- and second-generation Canadians, and members of visible minorities. They may get angry at governments that screw up, but they are not angry at elites per se. That's because for the most part, they are socially and economically aspirational: they would likely prefer their children grow up to join a club than a convoy. They are the type of voters who get excited not by the rabid talk of freedom but by the rational promise of opportunity.

This Convoy–Club fault line is the same split that Donald Trump exploited so effectively within the Republican Party in the United States. When Trump declared that he loved the poorly educated, it was not because he thought they were stupid. It was because they were vulnerable. Their lack of education meant they were increasingly excluded from the advantages of a post-industrial economy, where manufacturing jobs had been outsourced and automated, where industries like coal had been shuttered, and where Richard Florida's "creative class" was considered more valuable than ordinary "working people." Trump's "deplorables" (an ill-advised term coined by Hillary Clinton),[23] also saw immigrants and people of colour advancing while they fell behind. They had lost their foothold in the American Dream, and that exclusion made them angry.

That anger made them ripe for a champion. Trump fit the bill. While he may be a wealthy businessman, he was not a classy politician. He was a lout, an Archie Bunker on steroids. But that was his appeal. Archie wouldn't judge the excluded. He would feel their pain. And more than anything, the excluded wanted to be heard, to be understood, and ultimately, to stick it to the people who appeared to deny them the life they felt they deserved.

Those people had a name: liberals. In the US, they were embodied in the person of Joe Biden, the newly elected Democratic president. In Canada, they were incarnated in the person of Justin Trudeau, thrice-elected Liberal prime minister. On January 6, 2021, Trump's people came for Biden in Washington. On January 31, 2022, they came for Trudeau in Ottawa.

Lest you think this is hyperbole, the Conservative Party's significant pro-Trump leanings were confirmed a month later in a poll by Leger, which found that while only 19 percent of Canadians would vote for Trump over Biden if they could participate in the US election, that number more than doubled within the ranks of the Conservative Party. Forty-six percent of Conservative voters would choose Trump, compared to 3 percent of Bloc Québécois voters and 5 percent of Liberal and New

Democratic Party voters. Meanwhile, a staggering 86 percent of People's Party of Canada (PPC) voters would opt for Trump.

In some respects, this should be expected: the PPC attracts the same "pandemic libertarians" (a phrase coined by esteemed political and business strategist Jaime Watt)[24] and far-right elements that flock to Trump, while Conservatives might be likely to vote for Republicans no matter the nominee, since the party is the most right-of-centre US offering. While previous available polls are not broken down by party, they show a similar result in terms of national numbers: in 2004, 60 percent of Canadians would have voted for Democrat John Kerry, versus 22 percent for Republican George W. Bush and 2 percent for Ralph Nader. (Eight percent would have voted for none of the three, while 9 percent didn't know which nominee they would have voted for.)[25] In 2012, 86 percent of Canadians would have voted for Democrat Barack Obama and 14 percent for Republican Mitt Romney.[26] And in 2020, 80 percent of Canadians would have voted for Biden, 20 percent for Trump.[27]

What Republican voters are buying, however, has changed. Trump has transformed the party from one of conservative principles—Reagan's "shining city on a hill," Bush's neoconservatism—to a nativist movement rooted in grievances against immigrants and elites. That is arguably a tougher sell in an immigrant-dense country like Canada. By 2036, Canada will be a nation "as brown as it is white," with 30 percent of its citizens born outside the country,[28] migrating from Asia, South Asia, the Middle East, South America, and Africa. It is also a country where 80 percent of people live in cities. That number will increase in the coming decades; by 2046, for example, the horseshoe of growing communities around the Greater Toronto Area, from Niagara to Kitchener-Waterloo to Barrie will have 14.6 million people, up from ten million today.[29]

Politics, ultimately, is a numbers game. In our first-past-the-post Westminster system, you need the right number of votes in the right number of places to get a majority of seats and form the government. In the last two elections, the Conservatives won more votes than the Liberals, but the concentration of those votes in Western and rural ridings meant that the Liberals scored more seats. The key to breaking this deadlock is expanding the base in Eastern, suburban, and urban ridings—the very places Convoy Conservatives deride as liberal and elitist. The places where not only the Club Conservatives but a lot of Common Sense Canadians dwell.

Many of those Common Sense people were Tories in a previous life, and could be once more. They were my mainstream small-c conservative next-door neighbours in Toronto, who said after the CPC supported the convoy they could never vote for the party again. A long-time Conservative activist in Ottawa who called me and said he no longer recognized the political family he grew up in. Friends from Montreal and Calgary with whom I had been in the Progressive Conservative trenches thirty years ago who felt they no longer had a political home. And most importantly, their kids—the next generation of voters whom the Conservatives need to attract.

All is not lost, however. Before we lament that Canada will become nothing more than a Mar-a-Lago with snow, we should take stock of the situation. There are a lot of people in the Conservative Party who are mad as hell but don't see anger as the solution. There are a lot of Common Sense Canadians who believe in rights and responsibilities, uphold law and order, and want a brighter future for their families. They hate Trudeau but don't want to be tarred with Trump's brush. They might support the aims of the convoy but not the means. They don't subscribe to a perverted form of "freedom." And they want to build bridges, not walls.

If Conservatives intend to remain a vital force and potential governing party, they need to put aside their differences and build a winning coalition. That is going to require some soul-searching and self-examination. Canadian Conservatives need to ask themselves some fundamental questions, including: How did we get here? What is Canadian conservatism? And how can we unite, inspire, and take Canada forward—and win a majority government?

Some of that is already happening in the current leadership race. In the following pages, I will attempt to find more answers. Not just for the Conservative Party but for Canada as well. As someone who spent decades fighting for conservative policies and principles, it breaks my heart to see what could happen if the party cannot make peace with itself. When I started writing this book after the 2021 election, no one could have foreseen the events of 2022, including the convoy, the war in Ukraine, galloping inflation, and economic anxiety. In light of these, Canada needs strong leadership more than ever. I ultimately decided not to toss my hat in the Conservative contest, but did choose to support Jean Charest, who would bring what I feel is needed in a leader: gravitas, character, experience, and vision. It is not in the frame of a leadership partisan that I write this book, however, but as a Conservative partisan. I believe that Canada needs a choice of governing parties, and that conservatism offers a better path out of our present malaise than the current Liberal government. The Conservatives can be that choice but only if they can find some common ground. I hope this book offers the next leader, whoever he or she is, some guidance and insight into how to achieve this.

And it's not just up to the leader; everyone has a part to play. The Club Conservatives have to acknowledge the anger of the Convoy, even if they don't like to hear it. The Convoy Conservatives have to understand that a slide into Republican-lite populism would doom the party to perpetual opposition, and by extension, doom Canada to domination by the Liberals and the Left. Unless the factions can stop fighting, there is also the very real risk of the Conservative Party breaking up again, with more centrist Tories leaving the fold to form a new organization—which would potentially guarantee the Liberals free rein, like the election of the Reform Party did in 1993. None of these scenarios are appealing—at least not if we want to maintain a healthy, vibrant democracy with real choices that appeal to the Common Sense Canadian voter.

In other words, fellow Conservatives, we've got a lot of work ahead of us. So let's get to it.

CHAPTER ONE

THE HARPER YEARS:
RECASTING THE CANADIAN NARRATIVE

Before the Convoy, before the Club, there was a common-sense man named Stephen Joseph Harper. Raised in the leafy Leaside neighbourhood of Toronto, Harper came of age politically in Calgary and was first elected under the banner of the Reform Party. He would become the man to put Humpty Dumpty back together again, when he was elected leader of the new Conservative Party of Canada in 2003.

The CPC represented a merger of the Progressive Conservative Party of Canada and the Canadian Alliance. Contrary to the view of some members of the CPC, the party's history spans more than a scant twenty years; it can be traced back to the Liberal-Conservative Party of Canada's first prime minister, John A. Macdonald, in 1867. Historian Bob Plamondon, who has written several books on the history of the Conservative Party in all its iterations, describes Macdonald thusly:

"Though Macdonald was a Tory, he was not kin to the Big Business establishment Tories from Toronto. Instead, he admired William Henry Draper, the moderate conservative leader who sought to strengthen the party by reaching out to elements of French Canada . . . In Parliament, Macdonald fought extreme elements from both sides of the aisle.

Opposing annexation by the United States, or countering Tory elements that sought to assimilate the French, Macdonald stood for tradition."[1]

Plamondon also quotes Governor Lord Elgin who described Macdonald as "a respectable man, intolerably moderate in his views . . . who belongs to the section of the conservatives who are becoming reasonable."[2] Macdonald considered himself a "progressive conservative,"[3] though his party never bore that name.

In the ensuing hundred and fifty–odd years, Canada's conservative parties have sported different names and different brands. They have been shaped by Toryism, populism, and a variety of other isms along the way. The most successful ones, like Macdonald's, formed majorities thanks to national coalitions that brought together different types of conservatives, ethnicities, geographies, and interests under one big tent. This ability to unify has always proven crucial to taking and keeping power. When the coalition fractures, power is lost, and the so-called "Natural Governing Party"—a.k.a. the Liberal Party of Canada—takes the reins once more.

Early on in his political career, Harper, like Macdonald, saw the necessity of the big-tent approach. But unlike Macdonald, his tent was not based in geography or ethnic origin but in a citizen's relationship with the state. In 1989, Harper proposed this model for the Reform Party. Harper believed the party "should tailor its broader 'social' agenda to gain a sizable chunk of the urban-working-class and rural-sector 'swing' vote, without alienating its urban private-sector middle-class 'core.' The key is to emphasize moderate conservative social values consistent with the traditional family, the market economy, and patriotism."[4]

As author Paul Wells observed, the interesting thing about this model is that it does not give much leverage to social conservatives, as Harper was oft accused of doing. It depends more on believers in economic freedom, lower taxes, and small government. It also draws a distinct cleavage between lower-middle– and middle-upper–class voters, not due to their level of income, but to its source, being either the public or private sector.

In the words of then Reform advisor Tom Flanagan, "The older model of a conservative party based largely on the middle and upper classes is no longer viable, because so much of the urban middle class (for example, teachers, nurses, social workers, and public sector administrators) is now part of the 'new class,' or 'knowledge class,' as it is sometimes called, and is thus a political class dependent on tax-supported government programs. Political coalitions now divide less along class lines than on the question of public-sector dependence."[5]

Thirty years later, that same cleavage would manifest itself during the COVID-19 pandemic, which was experienced very differently by professional, knowledge, and public-sector workers than by tradespeople, small-business owners, and blue-collar and retail workers. Within the Conservative Party, it forms the basis of the divide between the Convoy and Club Conservatives. It explains the raucous standing ovations that greet Pierre Poilievre's frequent exhortations to "defund the CBC," considered by some in the party to be the ultimate symbol of government-funded media elitism.

But Harper's "Joe and Jane Lunchbucket" model for the Reform Party was never taken up. Instead, Reform leader Preston Manning built a movement rooted in geographic exclusion, coloured by anti-Quebec overtones and a demand for democratic reform. The party's 1993 election slogan was "The West Wants In!" It opposed official bilingualism and special status for Quebec and was endorsed in its early days by the neo-Nazi organization the Heritage Front and by the Alliance for the Preservation of English in Canada.[6] Not surprisingly, none of this won the party any love east of the Manitoba–Ontario border, where it only ever secured one seat.

Manning talked a great deal about direct, "bottom-up," and "grassroots" democracy. According to Manning, populism is the "common sense of the common people that would allow the public to have more say in the development of public policy through direct consultation, constitutional conventions, constituent assemblies, national referenda, and citizens' initiatives."[7] While the Reform Party was unquestionably populist, Manning was very uncomfortable with the label. He acknowledged populism's "dark side . . . whereby some demagogue bamboozles the public into support."[8]

By 1997, Harper had become disenchanted with the direction of Reform and left to head the non-partisan National Citizens Coalition.

A year earlier, at the Winds of Change Conference organized as part of the "Unite the Right" movement, he also changed his tune on the ingredients for a winning conservative coalition, recommending that a united conservative party harness "Quebec nationalists to Western populist conservatives to Ontario's Red Tories."[9] While he thought Mulroney had overreached by including separatists in his coalition, he otherwise believed that "the solution was to reunite the movement by offering a genuinely conservative party (the Reform part) but nonetheless accepting the wisdom of incremental change (the Tory tradition) and respecting Quebec's aspiration to be the master of its own destiny (Quebec nationalists)—while also respecting the rights of other provinces and regions."[10]

Four years later, when the successor party to Reform, the Canadian Alliance, began to founder under the leadership of Stockwell Day, Harper quit the NCC and signalled his interest in running for leader of the CA. Unlike Manning, his goal was to provide a clear voice for conservatism in Canada.[11] But the reality of the new party was already tilting that balance away from Progressive Conservative moderation toward reformist-style populism.

Harper handily won the leadership of the new party with 56.2 percent support under the hundred-points-per-riding system. His closest rival, Belinda Stronach, secured 34.5 percent. This would seem to indicate that the Progressive Conservative flank of the party, which had strongly supported Stronach, still had clout. But as author John Ibbitson notes, if you stripped away the points system, which skewed the vote in favour of candidates who won in ridings with lower membership counts, Harper had taken 69 percent of votes cast, while Stronach had taken 26 percent.[12] That 26 percent represented both Ontarian Red Tory and Québécois interests.

In other words, Harper's coalition was far from the egalitarian marriage he recommended in 1996. Reform–Alliance elements were already dominant and would become even more so in the years that followed.

Just weeks after taking the leadership, Harper and the new party were plunged into the 2004 election campaign. Liberal leader Paul

Martin, who took the helm of his party only a few months before, seized the occasion, expecting that the Conservatives weren't ready to fight a general election. He was right. Unfortunately for him, the Liberals weren't either. On the tails of the sponsorship scandal, Adscam, the Liberals barely eked out a minority, which would last all of eighteen months before it was brought down by a non-confidence vote. In that election, Harper and the Conservatives would come to power—and hold it for the next nine years.

The first Harper government was a minority that lasted until 2008; the CPC won 124 of 308 seats in 2006 but was outgunned by the Liberals in Ontario, Quebec, and Atlantic Canada. The Bloc had fifty-one seats, the NDP, twenty-nine. As writer John Ibbitson observed, "That meant the Liberals could defeat the Conservatives with the help of any other party."[13]

Despite this, Harper implemented several key parts of his agenda during his first term. The first was the Federal Accountability Act, a direct response to the Gomery Report on the sponsorship scandal. This act "banned corporate, union, and large personal political donations; imposed detailed monitoring on lobbying; provided additional protection for whistle-blowers; and enhanced the powers of the auditor general."[14] The government also enacted legislation to set a fixed election date provided it was not defeated on a vote of confidence in the House of Commons. As Plamondon notes, however, Harper violated the very spirit of that act when he called an early election in 2008.

Other pieces of legislation in Harper's first mandate addressed the so-called "fiscal imbalance" between Ottawa and the provinces, an issue high on Quebec's agenda. In November 2006, Harper further proposed a motion, "That this House recognize that the Québécois form a nation within a united Canada,"[15] after the National Assembly of Quebec had done the same earlier in the year. Not everyone agreed; Harper's minister of intergovernmental affairs, Michael Chong, resigned rather than support the motion. But coupled with obtaining a seat for Quebec at UNESCO, this was seen as a means of significantly increasing the Tories' dismal ten ridings in the province—a strategy that unfortunately never came to fruition.

One policy with enduring impact, however, was Harper's decision to cut two points from the goods and services tax (GST)—one in 2006 and another in 2007. This was both a popular campaign promise and a means of limiting the growth of the federal government. In the words of Laval University economist Stephen Gordon, the cuts "blew a $12 billion hole in the federal balance that will have to be filled somehow." Or, as author Paul Wells points out, left empty. "By 2010," Wells notes, "federal revenues as a share of GDP would hit their lowest level since 1963."[16] Less revenue meant less money for government to spend and play a larger-than-necessary role in the life of its citizens, one of Harper's central tenets.

While Harper's tax cuts shrunk the size of the state, one of the drawbacks was a shift from consumption tax to personal income tax, which from an economic standpoint is less efficient. It also limited the ability of the federal government to further reduce marginal effective rates of income tax.[17] Over the lifetime of Harper's government, he would also introduce other popular tax measures including "boutique" tax credits for things like children's sporting activities, as well as changes to the personal income tax system, such as income-splitting for parents with children under eighteen, introduced in 2014,[18] and the tax-free savings account (TFSA) in 2009.

These tax changes were not all about dollars and cents—there was a moral component to them as well. In 2003, Harper delivered a speech to the Civitas Society, an invitation-only gathering of right-of-centre thinkers, academics, and activists, in which he expounded on the importance of moral conservatism. In Harper's view, with the Left embracing more right-of-centre positions such as balanced budgets, the goalposts had shifted for Conservatives, and they needed to fight on this values-driven terrain.

"Conservatives need to reassess our understanding of the modern Left," he stated. "It has moved beyond socialistic morality or even moral relativism to something much darker. It has become a kind of moral nihilism—the rejection of any tradition or convention of morality, a post-Marxism with deep resentments, even hatreds of the norms of free and democratic Western civilization." Harper believed that Conservatives needed to talk about values and confront the liberal welfare-state threat to "our most important institutions, particularly the family."[19]

This conviction informed several pieces of legislation under Harper's government. These included the family-friendly tax credits already noted, as well as the Universal Child Care Benefit, introduced shortly before the 2015 election.[20] It also informed the creation of the Office of Religious Freedom, which spent much of its time assisting persecuted Christians in countries like China and Iran. And while Harper did not reopen the abortion debate, his initiative supporting maternal and child health refused to fund abortions overseas, which pleased social conservatives and which would be resurrected in the platform of pro-life candidate Leslyn Lewis in both the 2020 and 2022 CPC leadership races.

Another area where Harper infused legislation with a moral component was law and order. Harper implemented major changes to the justice system throughout his three terms. Between 2006 and 2011, his "Tough on Crime" agenda created five new offences related to street racing, raised the age of consent to sexual activity from fourteen to sixteen years, and adopted the Eliminating Entitlements for Prisoners Act, which stripped convicted criminals of the right to receive Old Age Security. He also focused on victims' rights, creating a national ombudsman's office for victims of crime, and passed the Standing Up for Victims of White Collar Crime Act, as well as the Protecting Victims from Sex Offenders Act, which allowed police to proactively use a national sex offender database to prevent sex crimes.[21]

After Harper got a majority in 2011, changes accelerated. Harper packaged the new legislation in an omnibus bill, the Safe Streets and Communities Act. This bill wrought many fundamental changes to Canadian law, particularly in sentencing. It established mandatory minimum sentences for drug offences, sex crimes, crimes against children, and some violent offences. It ended the policy of "least restrictive measures" for inmates, eliminated house arrest as a punishment option for many offences, and increased penalties under the Young Offenders Act. The Conservatives also limited parole eligibility in the case of multiple murders (a provision struck down in 2022 by the Supreme Court)[22] and, in response to the case of Rehtaeh Parsons, a Nova Scotia teenager who committed suicide after images of her being sexually assaulted were shared online,[23] criminalized the non-consensual distribution of online images.

While the moral convictions underpinning Harper's justice policies were clear, those of other measures were more obtuse. These included Harper's war on the mandatory long-form census, which his government abolished in 2010. The move generated the ire of dozens of strange bedfellows: the Canadian Association of University Teachers, the Canadian Association for Business Economics, various editorial boards, a spate of provincial governments, the Canadian Labour Congress, the president of the C.D. Howe Institute . . . and the list went on. The government had a hard time justifying the change on privacy grounds: only two complaints had been made to the privacy commissioner about the 2006 mandatory census, and twenty-two expressions of concern to Statistics Canada.[24]

Why the decision? "Census suspicion" was a long-standing grievance among American and British conservatives, who saw it as an overreach by the bureaucracy into the lives of citizens—in the words of columnist George Jonas, "to foster plans of social engineering."[25] Without census data, the theory goes, government cannot design large, morally nihilistic, society-transforming, tax-sucking projects. This suspicion of big government and its moral agenda, or lack thereof, finds its echoes in the conversation Conservatives are having in 2022 about cancel culture, gender education in schools, free speech on campus, and other cultural concerns.

Harper's stance against moral relativism informed his adversarial relationship with the press, whom Harper identified as promoters of the left–liberal consensus. Harper was convinced that whenever the mainstream media, or "MSM," criticized him, he was on the right side of the issue—and his supporters believed this as well. Ever since, Conservative politicians have been running against "the media party" as much as they have been running against the Liberals or the NDP.

According to veteran journalist Jennifer Ditchburn, the Harper government began to "manage" the press immediately upon taking office in 2006, mostly by curtailing the flow of information. Reporters were no longer given access to ministers at the conclusion of cabinet meetings; "in fact, the timing of the cabinet meetings was no longer publicized."[26] Bureaucrats no longer gave reporters background briefings on the legislation they were crafting. The government introduced "Message Event Proposals," or MEPs, which outlined the parameters of events, messages to deliver, and media desired—all of which was managed by the Communications and Consultation Unit within the Privy Council Office, and in the early years, by the prime minister's chief of staff.[27]

As a result, reporters turned to other sources for information about the government, including NGOs, think tanks, lobbyists, and even foreign governments. Access to information requests by the media shot up from 2,835 in 2003–2004 to 8,321 in 2012–2013, a 210 percent increase. And the CBC took a hit. Under Harper's government, funding for the state broadcaster stayed static, going from $1.063 billion in 2003–2004 to only $1.065 billion in 2013–2014. After taking inflation into account, this represents a decline of $220 million in ten years.[28] These cuts would be reversed in later years by the Liberal government of Justin Trudeau.

Other areas of public policy also got less attention in the Harper years; like his predecessors and successors, Harper set climate change targets that were not met. Unlike them, he pulled Canada out of an international climate treaty, the Kyoto Protocol. "The Kyoto Protocol does not cover the world's largest two emitters, United States and China, and therefore cannot work," stated Environment Minister Peter Kent in December 2011. "It's now clear that Kyoto is not the path forward to a global solution to climate change. If anything, it's an impediment."[29] Kent added that Canada produced "barely two percent" of global emissions and chastised the Chrétien government for signing the accord in 1997 with no intention of meeting its targets. The fact that Kyoto had killed Alberta oil sands projects in 2002 also undoubtedly still resonated with the Conservatives' Western base.

Another weak policy area was Indigenous issues. While Harper started his tenure on a positive note, offering an apology to former students of residential schools in 2008, his plans to increase funding for Indigenous education in 2014 collapsed when National Chief Shawn A-in-chut Atleo resigned from the Assembly of First Nations.[30] Harper also eliminated a number of programs, including the Aboriginal Healing Foundation, the National Aboriginal Health Organization, and Sisters in Spirit, an initiative related to the documentation of murdered and missing Indigenous women.[31] Harper's continued refusal to launch an inquiry into the issue prompted a spate of criticism from Indigenous groups, particularly after the discovery of the body of fifteen-year-old Manitoba Indigenous teen Tina Fontaine in August 2014.

Fontaine had been missing for over a month; fifty-three-year-old Raymond Cormier would later be charged with her murder but acquitted in 2018. Commenting on renewed calls for an inquiry, Harper stated that "it's very clear that there has been very fulsome study of this particular . . . of these particular things. They're not all one phenomenon . . . We should not view this as a sociological phenomenon. We should view it as crime."[32] Harper's statement refocused calls for his government to do more to address Indigenous issues.[33] They also gave an opening to his political opponents, including new Liberal leader Justin Trudeau, to paint the government as out of touch with a growing sympathy to First Nations concerns.

In 2013, Harper made similar statements following the foiling of a domestic terrorist plot to blow up a VIA train. "I think, though, this is not a time to commit sociology, if I can use an expression," Harper said. "These things are serious threats, global terrorist attacks, people who have agendas of violence that are deep and abiding threats to all the values our society stands for."[34] Again, Harper infused his condemnation with a call to uphold values, consistent with his view that they were under threat from multiple factors, be it terrorism or the creeping growth of "woke" culture.

Harper's remarks on sociology came a week after the Boston Marathon bombing and comments by Justin Trudeau that politicians needed to look at the root causes of this attack, which could happen "because someone who feels completely excluded . . . at war with society."[35] Cue the outrage from the Tories: Pierre Poilievre bluntly told then *Power & Politics* host Evan Solomon that "the root cause of terrorism is terrorists. That's how we respond."[36]

As the 2015 election approached, a clear divide was forming

between the Left and the Right in Canada on crime, political correctness, and other values-based issues. Terrorism made that list. In October 2014, a lone gunman, Michael Zehaf-Bibeau, killed Corporal Nathan Cirillo at the National War Memorial before rampaging through the House of Commons, wounding a House of Commons security guard, and sending MPs, including the PM, scurrying into closets, until Sergeant-at-Arms Kevin Vickers shot the gunman dead. Shortly thereafter, the Conservatives introduced Bill C-51, the Anti-terrorism Act, for which they were criticized not only for overreach on civil liberties but also for exploiting the attack for political gain.[37]

Harper's foreign policy was values-based as well. Harper was a staunch supporter of Israel, which represented a beacon of democracy and support for the West in the sea of autocracy and terror-friendly regimes that was the Middle East. Harper's unwavering support for the State of Israel won him many friends in that country, but lost him others at the United Nations, where Canada failed in its bid for a seat on the Security Council in 2010 and then elected not to run again for one in 2014.[38] (Six years later, under Trudeau, it would again fail to secure a spot.)

Harper's ultimate undoing came not because of policy but because of scandal. Despite starting off on an ethical high note with the Accountability Act and standing for moral values throughout his tenure, he finished his career as prime minister fighting off accusations of corruption linked to, of all things, improperly claimed Senate expenses. The chief transgressor was Conservative senator Mike Duffy, who had claimed ninety thousand dollars in living expenses deemed improper by a Senate audit committee. Duffy maintained that he had been told he could claim the expenses. He furthermore did not have the means to pay them back, so Harper's chief of staff, Nigel S. Wright, wrote Duffy a personal cheque to cover the amount. In 2013, when the payoff became public, Harper claimed he knew nothing of it; Duffy said the opposite. Senator Duffy eventually went to trial for fraud and breach of trust, for which he was exonerated in 2016; Wright was never charged.

This affair dragged on for months and did terrible damage to the government, destroying its reputation for ethics, one of the original pillars of its mandate in 2006. In June 2015, just months before the fall federal election, Auditor General Michael Ferguson released a report recommending that the cases of nine senators be referred for RCMP investigation, while twenty-one other senators were flagged for filing inappropriate expense claims. It was a final nail in the ethical coffin at the worst possible time.

Harper's legacy is mixed. In his nine years in power, he made a valiant and sustained attempt to recast the Canadian narrative in Common Sense Conservative terms. His policies were intensely values driven, from law and order, to economics, to foreign policy. He sought to cement the influence of Western Canada in Canadian affairs, not only through political means but through economic means as well. But events conspired against him: the Great Recession of 2008 plunged Canada back into deficit, the plummeting price of oil made oilsands projects less attractive, environmentalists fought the Keystone XL Pipeline both north and south of the Canada–US border, and relations with China, the potential purchaser of Canadian energy, frayed. Harper thus failed in his ambition to make Canada a "global energy superpower," a petrostate like no other, and thereby reverse the long-standing transfer of Western wealth to Central Canada. Instead, Harper left no major national legacy project, and much of his legislation was reversed by the subsequent Liberal government.

During his three terms in power, Harper's fortunes depended on a divided opposition. Harper had the luxury of facing two weak Liberal leaders, Stéphane Dion and Michael Ignatieff, and one strong NDP leader, Jack Layton. This combination helped split the left-of-centre vote to the Conservatives' advantage, notably in the 2011 election where Harper won a majority. The Conservatives' success with New Canadian voters (recent immigrants or "First Generation" Canadians born outside of Canada) in that election further cemented their victory in the all-important 905 belt around Toronto and gave the party hopes of establishing a permanent beachhead in immigrant communities.

In 2015, however, Harper faced a new foe at the ballot box. His name was Justin Trudeau. And if timing is everything in politics, Trudeau knew just when to make his entrance.

— CHAPTER TWO —

THE TRUDEAU YEARS:
FROM SUNNY WAYS TO
STORMY DAYS

When Justin Trudeau was elected leader of the Liberal Party of Canada in the spring of 2013, the party was in the dumps. The 2011 federal election had reduced it to a nadir of thirty-six seats and a dismal third place in the House of Commons. Stephen Harper's Conservatives had a majority government, while Jack Layton's NDP formed the Official Opposition for the first time in the party's history.

In contrast, after two lost elections and two lacklustre leaders, the Liberals were rudderless and diminished. Pundits openly speculated on the party's potential demise. *National Post* columnist Andrew Coyne opined that "the threat to the party is not that it might lose the next election, but that it might disappear altogether."[1] Author Peter C. Newman observed, "They have no power base . . . They've lost their Toronto fortress, their Maritime fortress, and Quebec fortress, and they haven't been out West in awhile."[2]

The big beneficiaries of the Liberals' troubles were seen to be the Conservatives. In their book, *The Big Shift*, published a few months before Trudeau became Liberal leader, authors John Ibbitson and Darrell Bricker predicted that Canada's political centre of gravity would shift westward due to immigration patterns that favoured growth in

Alberta and BC. They also saw in certain New Canadian communities the potential for sustained Conservative support in areas around the GTA and predicted that as long as the Conservatives could maintain a base of support of immigrants in coalition with Old Canada, and suburban Ontario in coalition with the West, the Tories could continue to win elections.[3] It helped that the influence of the Laurentian Elite was apparently on the wane. "They don't matter," Ibbitson and Bricker asserted. "The country has moved beyond their understanding."[4]

Then came Justin Trudeau.

In his book *Promise and Peril*, author Aaron Wherry said it best: "Indeed, it is not hyperbole to say there had never been a Canadian politician quite like Justin Trudeau."[5] Son of Canada's fifteenth prime minister, Pierre Elliott Trudeau, and Margaret Trudeau, the daughter of Liberal cabinet minister James Sinclair, the younger Trudeau was the Laurentian Elite incarnate, immersed from birth in a heady stew of politics, power, and privilege. Trudeau biographer John Ivison notes that Justin was toasted as a future prime minister at the tender age of four months by none other than US president Richard Nixon.[6]

Despite a professed aversion to politics, Trudeau eventually fell into its orbit. He first came to public attention with the eulogy he delivered at his father's funeral in 2000. Senior Liberals saw in him a future leader and proceeded to take him under their wing. He was well supported in his political journey by a group of key advisors, including university friend Gerald Butts and future chief of staff Katie Telford. And like his maternal grandfather, he displayed a great talent for retail politics, that ability to connect with ordinary people on the ground, as evidenced by his hard-fought win for both the party nomination and election to the House of Commons in the working-class riding of Papineau in Montreal, previously held by the Bloc Québécois.

All these elements positioned Trudeau not simply as an heir apparent, but as a saviour for a party that desperately needed saving. In April 2013, he handily won the Liberal leadership on the first ballot with 80 percent of the vote. Even faced with candidates of high calibre such as former astronaut Marc Garneau, it was never a contest. With his winning smile and famous name, Trudeau was the poster boy not only for Liberals' past but for Liberals' future. Like his famous father, he incarnated a zeitgeist of change.

Just as importantly, Trudeau was in many ways the opposite of Harper. Trudeau was suave where Harper was taciturn. He loved the press while Harper detested them. He spoke of "sunny ways" while Harper evinced a "dour, workmanlike character."[7] Trudeau had what British sociologist Catherine Hakim dubbed "erotic capital"[8] and he worked it to the hilt, posing for as many selfies as people would take. He was political royalty and—in the company of his equally telegenic wife and children—a Canadian version of John F. Kennedy. Media and voters lapped it up.

He also had a CV as thin as a fingernail. Prior to entering politics, Trudeau had worked stints as a drama teacher, a professional speaker, and a spokesperson for the youth program Katimavik. He had acted in a CBC miniseries. He had started a master's degree in environmental geography, but abandoned it to run for office. The Conservative brain trust took one look at this and tagged him as "just not ready," rolling out some very clever advertising spots featuring a group of mock employers tut-tutting over his CV, which promptly went viral online.

However, the same brains also made one fatal mistake. By holding a campaign of nearly eighty days, they gave Trudeau ample time to get ready. The Liberal leader crisscrossed the country doing what he did best: engage with voters. During his leadership run he perfected a particular "greet and grasp"—a double-hand clasp for women, and a firm grip on the shoulder for men.[9] His celebrity status and sunny demeanour contrasted with the seriousness—and dourness—of Harper's campaign. And polls started to shift.

Capitalizing on Trudeau's personal appeal, the Liberals rolled out a digital strategy that was second to none. Copying the playbook of President Barack Obama, they targeted voters across the country using high-tech internet ads. The impact of their strategy cannot be understated; much as he might loathe the comparison, Poilievre's slick and successful digital campaign for the 2022 Tory leadership greatly resembles Trudeau's heavy use of video and selfie culture.

Events conspired against the Conservatives. Midway through the campaign, the Syrian refugee crisis exploded into the public consciousness with a graphic photo of five-year-old migrant Aylan Kurdi face down and drowned on a Turkish beach. This prompted not only outrage about his death but concern about the government's intransigence in bringing Syrian refugees to safety. It took the Tories two weeks to even respond to the situation; by that time, the NDP had already pledged to bring in an additional ten thousand Syrians to Canada, while the Liberals pledged twenty-five thousand. Meanwhile, it emerged that of the ten thousand refugees the Conservatives had previously pledged to take, only 2,300 had actually been processed.[10] On the compassion metre, the score was Trudeau, one, Harper, zero.

Then, the Supreme Court issued a ruling overturning the federal ban on face coverings (such as the niqab) at citizenship ceremonies. The Conservatives had very vocally defended the ban and denounced the ruling. NDP leader Tom Mulcair and Liberal leader Trudeau both supported the decision, which had grave consequences for Mulcair in Quebec, a province whose previous Parti Québécois government had mused on banning face coverings for the public service. The NDP vote in "La Belle Province" cratered, opening an abyss that the Tories, Bloc, and Liberals sought to fill.

Smelling success, the Conservatives doubled down on what they saw as a wedge issue. On October 2, 2015, former ministers Kellie Leitch and Chris Alexander announced the Tories would create a tip line for "barbaric cultural practices," to report things like genital mutilation or forced marriage.[11] The tip line built on the Zero Tolerance for Barbaric Cultural Practices Act the party enacted in June of 2015, which established a minimum marriage age of sixteen, made polygamists inadmissible to Canada, and limited defences in cases of "honour killings" and spousal homicides.

While violence against women and girls is unquestionably abhorrent, a snitch line brings to mind communist dictatorships, not conservative values. Furthermore, coming on the heels of the niqab ban, the measure was seen as a veiled attack on Islam and an anti-immigrant dog-whistle. The effects were immediate and devastating.

A party report done after the 2021 election found that this policy cost the Tories significant support in the 2015 election, from voters in immigrant-heavy communities in BC and the GTA. "It did damage to the brand that we have not been able to resolve. We've never had the opportunity to rebuild the brand in cultural communities."[12] This torpedoed the New Canadian–Old Canada coalition that Ibbitson and Bricker identified as essential to keeping the Tories in power. In the words of Alexander, who contested the party leadership a year later, "it's why we lost . . . we allowed ourselves to be portrayed in the last election as unwelcoming. That was a huge mistake. It does make a lot of immigrants . . . nervous."[13]

The effects of the snitch line continue to reverberate six years later.[14] Candidates in the 2021 election, some of whom were visible minorities themselves, faced accusations that the party was intolerant. In a meeting of former GTA candidates held February 23, 2022, Daniel Lee, past candidate for Willowdale, who is of Korean descent, vividly recounted how he was called racist at the door when he went canvassing. Another former candidate, Maleeha Shahid of Whitby, who is Muslim, also reported similar experiences.[15]

In 2015, the mix of a rockstar Liberal leader, a tired and tarnished Conservative Party, and an NDP that lost Quebec produced a Liberal majority government. Trudeau was swept into power, and Harper promptly resigned.

Trudeau's promise of sunny ways, however, would start to fade over the next few years. Due to a combination of inexperience and arrogance, the PM and his team made multiple mistakes during their first term in office. And while he enjoyed a protracted honeymoon in terms of public opinion, Trudeau repeatedly found himself immersed in scandals large and small, which over time took their toll on Liberal support.

Initially, many observers accused Trudeau of overpromising: it would be simply impossible to completely fulfill, in four short years, the 353 commitments contained in the Liberal platform.[16] Faced with this challenge, Trudeau created the Results and Delivery Unit within the Privy Council Office in an attempt to implement "deliverology," a term coined by Sir Michael Barber, an advisor to the British government who led a similar unit for former UK PM Tony Blair.[17] By the end of his first term, according to researchers at Laval University, Trudeau had in fact kept 90 percent of his promises in some measure: 50 percent were completely fulfilled, 40 percent were partly fulfilled, and 10 percent were broken or not yet rated. The promises kept included signature commitments such as the Canada Child Benefit and Workers Benefit, environmental impact legislation, the legalization of cannabis, and the creation of the carbon tax.[18]

Nonetheless, it was the promises Trudeau broke that tended to make the headlines. Chief among those was the overarching promise to run "modest" deficits of roughly $10 billion a year over three years, before the budget returned to balance. Instead, Trudeau managed to tally up $94 billion in new debt over that period, and the budget was nowhere near balanced at the end of it.[19]

According to the Fraser Institute, between the Conservative government's last budget in 2015 and fiscal year 2018–2019, inflation-adjusted federal government program spending grew from $8,063 per person to $9,061 per person, the highest level in Canadian history up to that point. In 2019–2020, federal program spending rose further, setting a new record of $9,320 per person. After adjusting for inflation, it stood 3.6 percent higher than per-person spending levels during the 2009 recession. Fast forward to 2020 and the addition of COVID-related spending increased that number to $9,500 per person.[20]

The government justified this largesse with Trudeau's much-mocked rationale that "the budget will balance itself." It was true that if economic growth matched or outpaced spending growth, the rate of debt to GDP would stay steady or decline.[21] It was also true, however, that this demanded no fiscal discipline from the government; instead, Trudeau's government was free to treat tax revenue like a homeowner might treat a home equity line of credit. As long as one's house value goes up, the reasoning is, one can continue to borrow to make improvements, while the ratio of the loan to the house value goes down. But that also means that the debt never goes away—and if interest rates go up and house prices fall, or other calamities arise (such as, say, a worldwide pandemic), the homeowner can literally lose the roof over his head.

A second major policy fail in Trudeau's first term was electoral reform. On September 21, 2015, Trudeau tweeted, "As prime minister, I'll make sure the 2015 election will be the last under first-past-the-post system."[22] That changed after the government's Special Committee on Electoral Reform delivered its report in December of 2016. After extensive public consultations, the committee recommended that Canada adopt a proportional system of representation and put a proposal for such a change to a referendum.

Both ideas were anathema to Trudeau; for one, proportional representation would all but guarantee that coalition governments would become the norm, thus weakening the Liberals' hold on power, and a referendum would likely be a torturous affair doomed to failure, based on previous experiences in other provinces. Trudeau wrote off the experiment with the lame explanation that "there is no clear path forward . . . It would be irresponsible for us to do something that harms Canada's stability."[23]

The third big disappointment was his failure to fulfill his promise of reconciliation with Indigenous people in Canada. Taking a leaf from Brian Mulroney's playbook in 1984, when the Conservative leader promised to bring Quebec into the constitution "with honour and enthusiasm," Trudeau had similarly promised to rectify historical wrongs against Indigenous Peoples, an area Harper neglected. But as researchers Thierry Rodon and Martin Papillon observe, "Institutions that are a hundred and fifty years old cannot be changed in a matter of months."[24] While the two rate most of Trudeau's policies on Indigenous affairs as "kept in part," even those policies that were fully realized had mixed success.

Trudeau's National Inquiry into Missing and Murdered Indigenous Women and Girls, which Harper had refused to initiate, became bogged down in process disputes and internal wrangling. The 2015 Liberal pledge to end boil water advisories on reserves was still not fully realized six years later, when forty-two advisories remained in effect in thirty communities.[25] (The true number at any given time may be closer to one hundred, according to University of Calgary assistant professor and Canada Research Chair Kerry Black,[26] due to contaminants such as heavy metals and E. coli.) And Trudeau's government fought a human rights court ruling that would have had Ottawa compensate Indigenous children for the government's "wilful and reckless failure" to fund child and social services on reserves; as late as October 2021, the government appealed the decision[27] before finally settling with Indigenous communities and families for the sum of $31.5 billion in 2022.[28]

Apart from the broken and partly kept promises, there were also a host of poorly executed ones. One of these was cannabis legalization. Legalizing weed was one of Trudeau's signature promises in 2015, and a huge vote-getter. It appealed not only to young voters but to the medical cannabis community, which included swaths of soccer moms and aging boomers who turned to pot for anxiety relief or pain. When it came time to putting the promise into practice, however, it was a debacle. Legalization took effect July 1, 2018, imposing a Herculean timeline on provincial governments, who were responsible for implementation in terms of regulation, sale, law enforcement, and the like. While they bore the brunt of the public fallout, the botched job showed the weaknesses of a federal government that excelled at making sweeping promises but then "passed the buck" when it came time to execution.

Another Trudeau promise that fuelled discontent was the carbon tax. Again, it was a national pledge that demanded provincial action. Trudeau blithely announced the policy in October of 2016 and gave provinces less than two years to comply, stating, "If neither price nor cap and trade is in place by 2018, the Government of Canada will implement a price in that jurisdiction."[29] Cue the outrage in almost all jurisdictions apart from Quebec, which already had a cap-and-trade system in place. Even the NDP government of Alberta objected, with Premier Rachel Notley opposing the amounts set in the plan and countering that "we think it needs to happen concurrently with concrete action on energy infrastructure and in particular on getting a pipeline to tidewater."[30] That pipeline, of course, would later present another failure of the Trudeau government, when Kinder Morgan backed out of the Trans Mountain Expansion Project and the federal government ended up purchasing it for the sum of $4.5 billion.[31] As it turns out, it wasn't just Stephen Harper who couldn't get more oil to tidewater.

Even one of the big-ticket items that Trudeau did implement

failed to meet expectations. The Liberals' Canada Child Benefit was their more expansive—and expensive—counterpoint to Harper's policy of the same name. Enacted in the fall of 2015, the CCB was credited as early as 2017 with a full percentage-point drop in the national poverty rate, from 10.5 to 9.5 percent.[32] A year later, when he indexed the program to inflation,[33] Trudeau crowed, "The CCB is, I think, at the heart of everything that we promised to do . . . figuring out how to do work for the middle class and those working hard to join it, and how to make a real difference."[34]

But while the policy benefited low-income earners, it actually had some unintended negative consequences for the middle class. A study of the impact on dual-earner low- and middle-income households found very different outcomes for the two groups. Low-income households (defined for the study as dual-earner households where the main earner pulled in less than thirty thousand dollars a year) saw the income of secondary earners increase by an average of $1400 per year. These secondary earners, usually women, also increased their labour-force participation,[35] perhaps, theorized the study authors, because they could afford more childcare and thus work more outside the home.

The same, however, was not true of dual-earner middle-income households (defined as households where the main earner brought in thirty thousand to sixty-five thousand dollars a year). In these households, secondary earners' incomes actually *dropped* by an average of $2800 per year, and they experienced a decline in labour-force participation of 3.77 percent by secondary earners. The authors concluded, "For them, the CCB effectively acted as a leisure subsidy, dampening its ability to reduce child poverty." In other words, the CCB allowed parents to choose to work less rather than go out and earn more, though it's doubtful they spent this time engaged in "leisure," as any parent of young children will attest.

The policy outcome thus contradicted the government's assertion that the policy put the middle class further ahead economically. Other studies bear this out: overall, middle-class salaries *declined* by 0.2 percent during Trudeau's first term in office. In contrast, both the Liberal administration of Paul Martin and the three Tory terms of Harper had seen middle-class salaries grow, reaching their highest rates of growth, 3.9 percent and 3.7 percent, in Harper's last two terms in office.[36]

Yet this Child Benefit was touted—and widely seen—as helpful to the middle class. But if real economic gain wasn't the metric of success, what was? The answer is perception. In Trudeau's words, "Making a tangible difference both in people's lives and their day-to-day, but also in how they see their institutions, their government, and their future, as being invested in their success and part of their success—is at the centre of what I think we're trying to do in this whole thing."[37]

And thus the program may have achieved its political objective: positioning government as the friend of the coveted middle-class voter. It summed up the ethos of Trudeau's Liberal philosophy: voters could achieve security through government. It represented the opposite of Harper's vision, that of a citizenry less dependent on the state. Naturally, this irritated Conservatives who saw the changes they had fought for reversed. Well before the pandemic, vaccine mandates, the Canada Emergency Response Benefit, and truckers' protests, Trudeau had already set up the polarity between freedom and security that is playing itself out in the current CPC leadership race, in the cries for "freedom" that echo from the Convoy and their supporters.

Over his first four years in office, Trudeau's agenda to make government your friend exacerbated a problem that had been brewing since the 2008 Great Recession, and to an extent, the dot-com bubble of the late 1990s. That problem was the increasing disconnect between effort (defined as obtaining an education or training, working long hours, or multiple jobs) and result (being able to afford a lifestyle equal to or better than one's parents) for the middle class. The effects were being more strongly felt in the United States than Canada. According to a *New York Times* report released in 2014, "Median per capita income in the US has barely budged since 2000, while Canadians have seen their median income jump 20 percent."[38] But in 2015, the Liberal government acted as though Canada's middle class was in the same leaky boat as America's, creating a ministry of middle-class prosperity and a host of expensive programs designed to foster "equity" by transferring money to those lower down on the economic ladder.

Worse yet, the Liberal "solution" involved throwing large amounts of *borrowed* money at the putative problem. This racked up government debt, and made things even worse. And so despite doing all those "right things" we spoke of earlier, middle-class Canadians began to find themselves not further ahead—but further behind. Instead of achieving social mobility, they fell victim to social stagnation. A creeping sense of unfairness began to set in. And that unfairness underpinned the true legacy of the Trudeau years: the rise of populism.

CHAPTER THREE

TRUDEAU'S TRUE LEGACY:

STOKING THE WOKE

Compared to other countries this century, such as the UK and the United States, the modern wave of right-wing populism is late in coming to Canada. It is now, however, firmly entrenched in the People's Party of Canada, the Alberta-based Maverick Party, the Conservative Party of Quebec, and increasingly in the CPC. As in other nations, it is the product both of circumstance, including economic, industrial, and social dislocation, and leadership, both that of left-leaning politicians like Trudeau, who stoked the woke, and of right-of-centre politicians, who seized the opportunity.

As mentioned, Trudeau's time in office was marked by an astronomical growth of government. This growth predates the pandemic, where spending soared off the charts; from 2015–2019, it stemmed from both a philosophical perspective and a political calculation. Philosophically, it owed a debt to the ideas embodied in future minister-of-everything Chrystia Freeland's 2012 opus, *Plutocrats: The Rise of the New Global Super-Rich and the Fall of Everyone Else*. Freeland argued that the middle class was being "hollowed out" at the expense of the wealthy; she prescribed economic redistribution to remedy inequality. Politically, it sought to capitalize on middle-class voter anxiety. Trudeau followed

Freeland's advice and gave tax breaks to the middle class while raising taxes on the rich; he also pledged "more support to those working hard to join the middle class,"[1] playing to New Canadians' and working-class voters' desire for upward mobility. This, the Liberals figured, would win the support they needed to take key ridings in suburban Toronto, mainland BC, and suburban Quebec.

Mounting deficits, and the seemingly blasé attitude toward them, caused alarm for those who championed smaller government and lower taxes. Populist advocacy organizations like the Canadian Taxpayers Federation claimed Trudeau "broke their debt clock"[2] with his rising spending. The Fraser Institute declared that Trudeau had racked up more debt per capita than any prime minister since 1895 outside of world wars or economic downturn, rising from $30,922 in 2015 to $32,645 in 2019.[3]

In the 2019 election, both the Conservatives and the new People's Party of Canada jumped aboard the anti-debt bandwagon. The PPC promised to balance the budget within two years, while abolishing the capital gains tax and cutting personal income taxes to between 15 and 25 percent. The Conservatives pledged to balance the books in five years by taking a "measured approach to spending growth," and offered a host of boutique tax credits and a reduction in the lowest personal tax rate from 15 to 13.25 percent. The Liberals, for their part, stayed the course: they promised only to lower the debt-to-GDP ratio to 30.2 percent by 2023, from 30.9 percent in 2020–2022, while continuing to run deficits into 2023–2024. As for taxes, they promised to raise the personal exemption to fifteen thousand dollars but slap a luxury tax on pricey boats, cars, and planes.[4]

But the size of the state wasn't the only issue that ticked off right-of-centre voters: the Liberals' desire to right social wrongs was another. At the same time that Trudeau was expanding government, the issue of inequality surged to the public consciousness. #MeToo, Black Lives Matter, and Indigenous rights movements dominated the headlines, and the Liberals responded to increasing calls for social justice. Trudeau was already a fan of identity politics, having styled himself a feminist back in 2014 when he declared that the Liberal Party would tolerate no anti-abortion candidates,[5] and in 2015 when he kicked out two members of caucus over anonymous accusations of sexual harassment.[6] After he was elected prime minister, he famously declared that he was implementing gender parity in his cabinet "because it's 2015." He went on to bring in several feminist initiatives including the incorporation of gender-based analysis into the evaluation of federal policies and a gender-focused budget in 2018.

Author John Ivison describes Trudeau as having "an absolute conviction that Canadians share (his) devotion, bordering on dogmatism, for an activist agenda to transform Canada into a more egalitarian society by government fiat."[7] Ivison cites American conservative writer Thomas Sowell, who in 1995 penned a scathing critique of political correctness in which he distinguished between two groups: the "Anointed" and the "Benighted." According to Sowell, the Anointed have a "vision" wherein they predict future social, economic, or environmental problems unless the state steps in; they are deemed not merely correct (think Trudeau's reliance on "evidence-based policy"[8]) but morally superior. The Benighted are dismissed as "uninformed, irresponsible, or motivated by unworthy purposes" (think anti-mandate protesters during the convoy).

In the United States, the conflict between these groups would eventually play itself out in the 2016 fight between the elites and the deplorables which carried Donald Trump straight into the Oval Office. Trump famously declared "I love the poorly educated!"—and for good reason. Trump's audience felt that the elites held them in contempt, deeming them ignorant, unsophisticated, and bigoted. Trump supporters suffered through the global financial crisis and ensuant Great Recession of 2009, and many never recovered. Their manufacturing jobs had melted away, either shipped overseas or replaced by automation. Their economic mainstays, including coal and fossil fuel production, were under attack by environmentalists and regulators. They saw a rising urban class that included Asians, Blacks, Hispanics, and other non-white groups, while they, exurban or rural whites, languished. And for eight years, a Black man was their president.

In his 2016 book, *A Black Man in the White House*, American author Cornell Belcher describes it bluntly: "We are bearing witness to the truth of American politics—nothing trumps tribalism. While not the absolute or only variable, race is by and large the great political organizing line in America."[9] Belcher argues that many white Americans, specifically Republican white Americans, were unable to accept a Black man in the Oval Office.

Belcher is not the only scholar to conclude this; economist and professor William A. Darity Jr. told CBC's *As it Happens* that "unfortunately, I think the substantive consequence of his presidency will be the rise of the Trump regime."[10] Darity Jr. believed that it was Obama's failure to openly confront racism that produced this outcome, but other observers believed the mere fact that he won and kept power was enough. Former Democratic president Jimmy Carter told CNN media personality George Stephanopoulos: "I think . . . in a strange and I'd say unpleasant way, this kind of resurrected some animosity among people who are white and thought that whites should be superior."[11]

In what is perhaps the ultimate political paradox, Trudeau proved to be Canada's Obama. On the surface, the two leaders were polar opposites: Obama grew up with no social advantages, the son of a single mother, yet became editor of the *Harvard Law Review*, was hailed as brilliant by almost everyone who met him, and broke the ultimate glass ceiling by becoming the first Black president of the United States. Trudeau was born with a silver shovel in his mouth, the son of a sitting prime minister, yet was the consummate underachiever until he entered politics. But on their first visit, "Obama saw Trudeau as a kindred spirit" and "all but passed the baton to Trudeau as the defender of the liberal economic order."[12]

Like Obama, Trudeau was a champion of the woke ideal. He was the antithesis of Harper; he believed in making a better world through the will of government. But unlike Obama, who incarnated the values he defended, Trudeau was seen as a hypocrite who preached one thing but practised another. Trudeau championed gender equality but stood accused of groping a female reporter in British Columbia in August 2000.[13] He claimed that "diversity is our strength" but had donned blackface on multiple occasions. He said that Canada's relationship with First Nations "was its most important" and yet he threw the first Indigenous woman to be appointed attorney general and minister of justice, Jody

Wilson-Raybould, under the bus in the SNC-Lavalin scandal. He spoke of middle-class values yet vacationed on the Aga Khan's private island in the Bahamas, breaking ethics rules to boot.

Trudeau was also sanctimonious. If you disagreed with him, you were not only wrong, but a bad person. He, the Anointed, would not seek to enlighten the Benighted but shame them. And in doing so, he would sow a legacy of division and backlash.

Trudeau's contempt was on full display at a 2018 town hall in Sabrevois, Quebec, where he was heckled about his refugee policy and lack of border controls. Trudeau stood accused of encouraging migrants to cross illegally from the US to Canada at Emerson, Manitoba, and Roxham Road, Quebec, when he tweeted in response to Trump's Muslim immigration ban, "To those fleeing persecution, terror and war, Canadians will welcome you, regardless of your faith. Diversity is our strength #WelcomeToCanada." Trudeau's message was shared four hundred thousand times on Twitter and two hundred thirty-five thousand times on Facebook. Trudeau responded to the Sabrevois heckler by declaring that her "racism" had no place in Canada.[14]

As it turned out, the heckler in question was in fact linked to the Storm Alliance, a far-right group. But her concern about Canada's porous borders was shared by many Canadians who were not racist but angry that their country was allowing people to queue-jump while other refugees played by the rules. The PM's off-the-cuff, holier-than-thou response also sparked the resurrection of every blackface meme of Trudeau ever created. A similar outrage erupted in 2020, when the PM took a knee at a Black Lives Matter protest on Parliament Hill in 2020;[15] he was slammed from the Left and the Right for his "hollow gesture" that disrespected the RCMP that had protected him "since infancy."[16] Again in 2022 when he described unvaccinated people as "racists and misogynists" on a Quebec television program, the public responded indignantly.[17]

Trudeau also managed to antagonize social conservatives. In 2018, under Trudeau's watch, the Canada Summer Jobs Program announced that it would deny funding to groups unless they formally attested that their mandate respected the right to access safe and legal abortions.

Most of these groups were nowhere near the front line of abortion: they included summer camps, children's programs, and church groups. Trudeau's requirements resulted in one thousand five hundred rejections, with many of those groups refusing to sign attestations.[18]

That same year, when Conservative MP Lisa Raitt questioned the Liberals' putative commitment to gender equality, Trudeau's finance minister, Bill Morneau, responded that the government would "drag along the Neanderthals" who did not agree with the promotion of women into leadership roles.[19] For social conservatives, it recalled the moment they were mocked as "dinosaurs" in the 2000 election, when Liberal strategist Warren Kinsella famously whipped out a stuffed Barney doll to mock Canadian Alliance leader Stockwell Day, a move that helped secure another Liberal victory and left social conservative voters seething.

To complete the trifecta, Trudeau managed to enrage Western Canada, even more than his father had with his infamous National Energy Program. First, Trudeau imposed a carbon tax; next, he declared that oil and gas had to be phased out; finally, he brought in Bills C-48 and C-69 that hamstring resource development. At the same time, he incensed environmentalists by buying a pipeline when Kinder Morgan backed out of the Trans Mountain Expansion Project, and by failing to meet Canada's targets under the Paris Agreement.

In short, Trudeau paved the way for a populist opposition to take hold. And then came the COVID-19 pandemic.

In the past two years, the pandemic has reshaped politics around the globe. It accelerated trends that were already present, including populism and political polarization. Faith in government eroded and trust in the press cratered.[20] Authoritarianism is on the march, while democracy is in retreat.

Here in Canada, observers initially believed that government responses to the pandemic would reignite a love of big government— and some still do.[21] As the virus tore through populations, prompting lockdowns and shuttering businesses, government supports were often the only thing keeping people out of destitution. The Liberals rolled out benefits such as the CERB and its successor, the CRB, which enabled many Canadians to weather the storm. These measures also had negative effects, however, such as creating a shortage of workers in businesses where benefits actually exceeded wages.[22] But for many individuals, they reaffirmed faith in the state—and gave them a reason to vote Liberal.

This was borne out in the 2021 federal election. Research among Liberal voters done by the public affairs firm Navigator revealed that Canadians who voted Liberal did so overwhelmingly because of a sense that the Liberals cared about their well-being.[23] In focus groups, these voters said they felt the Liberals had been "there for them" during the pandemic and "had their interests at heart." Some went with "the devil they knew" because they did not trust the Conservatives to look out for them in the same way. The sense was that the Liberals "got it," on issues ranging from personal support to climate change. Thirty-three percent of voters agreed and brought the Liberals back into office with a minority government.

But in that same election, 34 percent of voters chose a different option: the CPC. An additional 5 percent chose the PPC. Both parties represented smaller-government choices, offering less spending and a road to budget balance. However, they had stark differences between them on things like climate policy, vaccine mandates, and gun control.

There is no question that the pandemic exacerbated political division. It also increased division on several other metrics. One of the main ones was work—specifically, whether you could work from home.

Soon after COVID-19 hit, it became apparent that Canadians were not "all in this together." The pandemic created two classes of workers: those who could work from home, and those who could not. WFH types were chiefly white collar, employed in professional sectors such as law, communications, and tech. They were in government and administrative sectors. They were generally better educated, better paid, and enjoyed access to technology. Many actually saw their disposable incomes rise as their costs of commuting or eating out went down.[24]

And while lockdowns were unpleasant, many of these workers came to appreciate being able to work from anywhere—including cottages, remote locations, and the like. Suddenly the office was less attractive. They began demanding hybrid options combining in-person days with WFH. Employers realized that they could save money through Zoom calls rather than in-person meetings, particularly for teams who had to travel to get together. It is safe to say that for white-collar workers, work will never be quite the same.

The same cannot be said for Canadians who could not work from home, such as retail workers, people in the trades, people in the performing arts, small-business owners, and essential workers in health, education, and front-line services. There was a divide even within these categories. Essential workers had to stay on the job, but those employed in non-essential services could not. Small businesses like hair salons and gyms were shuttered; restaurants could not seat diners; theatres could not receive patrons.

This combination of essential, creative, entrepreneurial, blue-collar, and unskilled workers suffered far more than their white-collar counterparts. American urban studies expert Joel Kotkin, who has written extensively about the plight of the working class, quotes epidemiologist Martin Kulldorff in a piece published this spring by the *National Post*: "Lockdowns have protected the laptop class of young, low-risk journalists, scientists, teachers, politicians, and lawyers, while throwing children, the working class, and high-risk older people under the bus."[25]

This is not a phenomenon unique to Canada. Around the globe, working-class people were kept from employment by government fiat, or they braved a higher risk of COVID when they were allowed back on the job. Working conditions were also more unpleasant as personal protective equipment a.k.a. PPE became the norm, as did the stress of dealing with clientele who may or may not respect mask restrictions, distancing, and other rules. The working class may well have felt that they lost control of their lives—a fact that the Poilievre campaign hits on in its messaging in the current CPC leadership race.

Another social divide reared its head at the same time: housing affordability. Despite a dramatic slowdown in immigration, which in theory should have eased the demand for housing, the price of homes in Canada skyrocketed.[26] Buoyed by low interest rates, fearful of COVID, and seeking more space, Canadians engaged in a frantic race to buy homes, especially in the suburbs, cottage country, and parts of Canada that had historically been relatively inexpensive, such as rural Ontario and Atlantic Canada.

Who was buying these homes? Again, a class divide emerged. Work-from-home professionals who could relocate to any community with WiFi upped and left the cities to buy up rural properties. Younger buyers of a wealthier cohort turned to the Bank of Mom and Dad for down payments. Investors snapped up properties as well. According to a report Statistics Canada published in April 2022, "multiple-property owners accounted for 31 percent of all homes in Ontario as of early 2020 and almost the same share in British Columbia . . . in the smaller East Coast provinces of Nova Scotia and New Brunswick, the share was about 40 percent."[27]

In 2022, the Trudeau government responded with a series of budget measures designed to cool the market, including a two-year ban on foreign ownership. The Bank of Canada also began hiking interest rates, which has begun to have an impact. Despite these efforts, housing inequity remains a rallying cry for millennials, Gen Z, and to an extent, their frustrated parents, who see their adult children unable to buy a home and instead, living in their basements. In a country like Canada, where home ownership is somewhat of a holy grail (at least compared to nations in Europe and Asia), 63 percent of non-homeowners have now "given up" on ever owning a home.[28] Combined with rising inflation and high gas prices due to the war in Ukraine, the housing "crisis" has made the cost of living the pre-eminent political issue of the day.

Finally, the impact of the pandemic divided itself on regional lines. Provincial governments took very different approaches to pandemic restrictions, with Quebec bringing in some of the harshest (such as curfews) while Alberta had arguably the most laissez-faire. Ontario's government took what was criticized as a flip-flop approach, particularly frustrating parents of younger children by continuously changing rules on school openings.[29] Atlantic Canada saw very low waves of COVID initially as it restricted travel from other parts of Canada.

Not surprisingly, public mood about the handling of the pandemic varied greatly across the country. The greatest dissatisfaction with provincial and federal plans was found in Alberta, followed by Manitoba, Saskatchewan, and Ontario, while the highest satisfaction was in Quebec, Atlantic Canada, and BC.[30]

Canada's new populism is rooted in these divides of worker class, economics, generations, and geography. It is reflected in Canadians' divergent attitudes toward the convoy that we examined earlier in the introduction. In the Conservative leadership race, this battle between populism and conservatism is playing out in a proxy fight between Poilievre and Charest. Poilievre attacks elites and pledges to fire gatekeepers, including the governor of the Bank of Canada. He extols the virtues of cryptocurrencies and "the freedom for buyers and sellers to choose Bitcoin and other technology."[31] He bashes the "COVID control freaks"[32] and demands an end to all vaccine mandates. In contrast, Charest offers a centre-right vision grounded in traditional conservative principles including fiscal responsibility and law and order. The two men diverge completely in their attitude toward the convoy, with Charest accusing Poilievre of supporting an "illegal blockade."[33] Charest's calling card is unity; his work fighting for the "No" side in the 1995 Quebec referendum is the reason that both men still have a country to lead.

The two candidates speak to different life experiences and present very different worldviews. As we will see in the next chapter, this wouldn't be the first time in Canadian history that such a divide has appeared in Conservative ranks. Canadian conservatism has flirted with populism before. It has danced with "funny money" theories; it has fed off Western alienation; it has channelled rage against the elites. And in 2018, even before the pandemic, one man saw this divide coming again and thought that for the Conservatives, the populist wave might actually be a good thing.

His name was Stephen Harper.

CHAPTER FOUR

POPULISM IN CANADA:
EVERYTHING OLD IS NEW AGAIN

In his 2018 book *Right Here, Right Now: Politics and Leadership in the Age of Disruption*, Stephen Harper discusses the rise of populism in Western democracies. Written before the pandemic, Harper observed that one of the key reasons Trump came to power is free trade and acknowledged that millions of workers in advanced economies experienced wage stagnation and job losses as a result.[1] He discusses how the World Economic Forum in Davos, Switzerland, has become a preserve of the elite—now serving as fodder for the anti-WEF sentiment raging in populist circles.[2] He describes the cleavage between the "Anywheres," the class of global and "globalist" workers who eschew nationalism in favour of mobility and trade, and the "Somewheres," whose lives are rooted to place, who depend on a local economy and social life, and who thus rely on a strong nation-state. And he describes what he himself practised while in office as "populist conservatism."

Harper defines populist conservatism as "putting conservative values and ideas into the service of working people and their families. It is about using conservative means for populist ends."[3] Harper believes it would be as wrong to double down on "unbridled populism" as it would to return to "supply-side" conservatism, which favoured the wealthy.

Rather, it is about applying conservative principles to populist concerns of the working and middle class.

Harper claims this is not about proposing a new form of conservatism but about rediscovering conservatism. Is it, though? Conservatism was a reaction to the revolution that swept away the monarchy of eighteenth-century France. It was born of a desire for incremental change, respect for tradition, and a refusal to cede to the excesses of revolutions—and the terror that inevitably accompanied them. Conservatism was a reaction *against* populism, which saw the very working people Harper champions revolt against the elites in radical and tumultuous ways.

Canadian conservatism is also a different beast than American or British conservatism. This is due to various factors, one of which is the structure of the country and its political system. Unlike the UK, which is a unitary state, Canada is a federation of ten provinces and three territories. Unlike the United States, which is a republican system dominated by two parties, Canada employs the Westminster parliamentary system, which allows for a multiplicity of parties. And unlike both the US and the UK, Canada is composed of two founding peoples and has two official languages.

Populist waves have thus produced a different outcome for Canadian conservatives than in those two countries, and could be expected to again. Chief among these outcomes is the creation of new parties at both the provincial and federal level, and a consequent splitting of the right-of-centre vote. While this has produced parties that have won power provincially, most notably in BC and Alberta, on the federal scene this has favoured the election of the Liberal Party, to the detriment of its Conservative opposition.

Only two parties have historically led federal governments in Canada: the Liberals and (due to a series of name changes) the Liberal Conservatives / Progressive Conservatives / Conservatives. There have been many other parties that have come and gone, fuelled by populism of both the Right and Left. These include the Progressives, whose high-water mark was the election of fifty-eight MPs in 1921 and who would merge with the Conservatives in 1948 to create the Progres-

sive Conservative Party; the Co-operative Commonwealth Federation, precursor to the NDP, that existed between 1932 and 1961;
Social Credit, 1935–1993, and its offshoot, the Ralliement créditiste,
1963–1971; and of course the Reform Party, which morphed into the
Canadian Reform Conservative Alliance in 2000 before becoming the
modern Conservative Party in 2003.

The current fight for the Conservative Party's soul is often depicted
as a legacy battle between the PC and Reform elements of the party. That
short-sighted view is likely a product of equally short political memo-
ries. The Progressive and Social Credit parties are not often discussed in
Conservative circles, but they certainly should be in order to understand
the situation of the current Conservative Party. Their rise and fall both
illustrate the challenges that conservatism has faced in Canada when
confronted with populist elements, and help explain where the Conservative Party finds itself today.

The Progressive Party combined agrarianism, populism, and
American progressivism. It began as a farmers' movement and resisted
the type of formal party structure that may have given it a better shot
at power at the federal level.[4] Its apex was the 1921 election, in which
it won twenty-four of the eighty-one federal seats from Ontario. It lost
most of those in the general election four years later. It did, however,
conserve most of its seats in the West. As it slowly dissolved over the
years, the Progressive Party's membership split three ways, with some
forming the "Ginger Group" (which eventually morphed into the CCF
and then the NDP), the bulk returning to the federal Liberal Party (who
had nicknamed the Progressives "Liberals in a hurry"), some merging
with the Conservative Party in 1942, and still others turning to the
Social Credit party.

Social Credit's platform was based on the monetary theories of
Clifford Hugh Douglas, a British engineer who lived between 1879 and
1952.[5] Douglas conducted a study of British companies and found that
workers were paid less in salaries and dividends than the value of the
goods and services they generated; in other words, the workers were not
paid enough to buy back what they had made. Douglas believed that this
led to inflation which eroded purchasing power. He proposed a solution

whereby workers would be paid a "dividend" in the form of a "social credit" that would bridge the gap between their remuneration and the value of what they produced. Douglas, a religious man, did not just view his policies as monetary but also as a type of "practical Christianity," to allow man the greatest amount of freedom to pursue his relationship with God.

In Alberta, a preacher by the name of William "Bible Bill" Aberhart became enamoured of Douglas's philosophy and founded the provincial Social Credit Party. Aberhart led the party to victory in 1935 and remained premier until his death in 1943. Faced with the ravages of the Great Depression, Aberhart proposed a solution to the lack of purchasing power and rampant inflation whereby the state would pay every Albertan a "credit"[6] of twenty-five dollars a month to "purchase the bare necessities of food, clothing, and shelter, whether he works or does not work, and he will never be asked to pay it back." This credit would be "issued by the provincial credit house instead of by the banks."

Aberhart's goal was to "prevent the evil effects of uncontrolled inflation or deflation." For constitutional reasons, his policy was never implemented and was instead widely derided as "funny money." While different from the monetary reforms championed by Poilievre in the current leadership race, the two find common ground in that both view "elites"—whether capitalists, bankers, or government bureaucrats—as the problem, depriving the working class of the wages due to them or eating their wages through inflationary policies. Just as Western Social Credit voters were receptive to the idea that the monetary system had to be reformed to make it more equitable, Poilievre supporters embrace the notion that monetary system reform is necessary to protect purchasing power and return control of money to the people, including alternatives like cryptocurrency.

Alberta elected Social Credit governments from 1935 to 1971 under Aberhart and his successor, Ernest Manning. In BC, the provincial Social Credit Party governed for all but three years between 1952 and 1991, under the premiership of W. A. C. Bennett, his son Bill Bennett, and Bill Vander Zalm. Federally, the Social Credit Party started off with seventeen seats in 1935, dropping to between ten and nineteen in subsequent elections, until 1958 when Progressive Conservative prime minister John Diefenbaker swept to power on his own populist wave, wiping out all their seats. Rebounding to thirty seats following Diefenbaker's defeat in 1962, the Socreds finally lost their last three seats in 1968. The Créditistes, Quebec's version of Social Credit, managed to continue winning seats for another three elections, until 1979, but then were routed as well.

As the federal Social Credit Party's fortunes faded in the 1960s, Ernest and Preston Manning encouraged a merger with the Progressive Conservatives led by Robert Stanfield, but it was not to be. Preston Manning describes this experience in his most recent book,[7] *Do Something!*, characterizing the period as one of the "critical times" of political realignment of Canadian conservatism, together with the creation of the Saskatchewan Party in 2007 and the United Conservative Party of Alberta in 2016. Manning remarks,

"It should be noted that in each of these instances of realignment, the changes involved were bitterly and vehemently opposed at the outset by the defenders of the status quo, only to be grudgingly accepted with the passage of time. Much needless expenditure of political energy and internal bickering could be avoided in the future if Conservatives were to accept that these periodic realignments are not eccentric 'one-off' disruptions of the political status quo to be feared and resisted but an essential feature of the evolution of Canadian conservatism to be cautiously welcomed, carefully managed, and gradually embraced."[8]

If the current 2022 leadership race is any indication, embracing each other is the last thing on the leading candidates' minds. The race has devolved into a gladiatorial combat, both in the arena of party debates and social media. It brings to mind the enmity between the Reform and PC camps in the 1990s, which took thirteen years and three lost elections to resolve.

As Adam Daifallah and I wrote in *Rescuing Canada's Right*, a popular myth is that Reform was created solely in response to Western discontent with Mulroney's Progressive Conservative government. Preston Manning had in fact long foreseen the genesis of a new party; in 1967, he helped his father, Ernest, pen a book called *Political*

Realignment: A Challenge to Thoughtful Canadians. It posited a set of ideas called "the social conservative position," which the Mannings wanted to see adopted by the federal Progressive Conservative Party. As noted, that merger attempt foundered. Failing that, the Mannings did not rule out creating a new party, which is what ended up happening with Reform.[9]

Populism did not always spawn new parties, but it did take the Progressive Conservative Party in new and sometimes highly successful directions. This happened under the watch of John Diefenbaker in 1957. Diefenbaker was the first—and still the only—prime minister with a surname not of French or English extraction. He was a fiery orator who took the Conservative Party to victory in 1957 with a coalition spanning the West and Quebec.

"Diefenbaker knew that to win he needed more of the natural Tory supporters in the country," writes historian Bob Plamondon. "In the previous five federal elections, the best the party had mustered in the popular vote was 30.3 percent. The Tories needed a way to attract and motivate the undecided, the apathetic, and the disenchanted to the Tory side. The key was the populist Diefenbaker. He appealed to the average Canadian: "My abiding interest is your interest; my guiding principle is the welfare of the average Canadian." "It's time for a Diefenbaker government" was the Tory campaign slogan in 1957."[10]

Diefenbaker promised to cut taxes, boost pensions, restore parliamentary sovereignty, develop Canada's resources, turn "tight money" loose and reverse a housing slump. He appealed to farmers with a pledge to make advance cash payments on farm-stored grain; he promised to give more money to provinces and municipalities; he vowed to pursue free trade with the Commonwealth.[11]

In Diefenbaker's words, "It is a program . . . for a united Canada, for one Canada, for Canada first, in every aspect of our political and public life, for the welfare of the average man and woman. That is my approach to public affairs and has been throughout my life . . . A Canada, united from coast to coast, wherein there will be freedom for the individual, freedom of enterprise and where there will be a government which, in all its actions, will remain the servant and not the master of the people.[12]

If these words sound familiar, they should; Poilievre sprinkles them liberally into his speeches and references Diefenbaker by name. For the Tory leader, they were the product of lived experience. In a 1977 interview with the CBC, Diefenbaker described witnessing injustice against French Canadians, Indigenous people, and the Métis—and felt it himself, being referred to as "a Hun" when he ran for the Saskatchewan legislature in 1925, which he did not win. He was also not beloved by the Conservative establishment, who supported George Drew during Diefenbaker's first leadership bid in 1948; Drew won the crown but lost the subsequent election.

"From my earliest days, I knew the meaning of discrimination," recalled Diefenbaker. "Many Canadians were virtually second-hand citizens because of their names and racial origin. Indeed, it seemed until the end of World War II that the only first-class Canadians were either of English or French descent. As a youth, I determined to devote myself to assuring that all Canadians, whatever their racial origin, were equal and declared myself to be a sworn enemy of discrimination."[13]

During his tenure, Diefenbaker appointed the first female cabinet minister, Ellen Fairclough, and the first Indigenous member of the Senate, James Gladstone. He removed discriminatory immigration laws and granted the vote to First Nations and Inuit Peoples. Diefenbaker is also remembered for the Bill of Rights and his stance against South Africa's apartheid policy. "Dief the Chief" went on to win two more elections, a historic majority in 1958 and a minority in 1962, before falling to defeat in 1963.

Diefenbaker is also remembered for less salutary events, including a dust-up with the governor of the Bank of Canada over monetary policy, and sour relations with the United States, spurred by his opposition to equip Canada's newly-purchased Bomarc missiles with nuclear warheads. Under Diefenbaker's watch, the Progressive Conservatives also failed to establish a long-term presence in Quebec and lost urban support; in fact, as we will see in a later chapter, this marked the beginning of a consistent decline in Conservative fortunes in Canada's urban centres.

If the next Tory leader were to seek to replicate Diefenbaker's success by taking the Tories in a populist direction, there is one other parallel to draw. Just as the Progressive Conservatives saw the populist Social Credit Party as a threat in the 1950s, the Conservatives see the People's Party of Canada as siphoning off populist votes in 2022. The difference, of course, is the size of the threat: the Socreds had almost twenty seats in Parliament in 1957—the PPC lost their only one in the 2021 election. Still, the party garnered 5.1 percent of the national vote in that contest, enough to deny victory to at least six Conservative candidates and possibly more. PPC candidates got between 4 and 11 percent of the local vote in various ridings, for a total of 814,547 votes, up from 1.6 percent of the national vote and a total of 292,661 votes in 2019.[14]

The growth in PPC support can be directly attributed to the COVID-19 pandemic and its ensuant issues: frustration with lockdowns, vaccine mandates, and mask restrictions. Leader Maxime Bernier, who founded the PPC in 2018 after losing the Conservative leadership to Andrew Scheer, has prided himself on being unvaccinated and has also spoken out against vaccines. During the 2021 election campaign, Bernier hosted large rallies and talked at length about freedom. A profile of Bernier in the *Washington Post* notes a comparison to Donald Trump and describes his voter demographic as mostly male, working class and under fifty, staunchly opposed to vaccines, and "heavily influenced by disinformation from social media," according to Frank Graves of EKOS Research.[15]

Also in that election, the PPC attracted some far-right elements that were later on display at the convoy, including COVID-19 conspiracy theorists. In a CTV interview the day after the election, Evan Balgord, executive director of the Canadian Anti-Hate Network, said that "the COVID-19 pandemic was a gift to the Far Right" as it allowed them to infiltrate conspiracy theory spaces and begin attracting new followers. "The rise of the party kind of fit into this because these people didn't really have a political party. If they voted for any party, they would vote Conservative," he said. "But they weren't particularly happy about voting Conservative either, because they're the most fringe. So when the PPC started as a party in 2019, Bernier, right from day one, was using their language, their talking points, and the words of the Far Right in several spaces. We saw them actually say 'Bernier is dog-whistling to us.'"[16]

Should the Conservatives take a right turn and a populist bent to attract PPC voters? Bernier is clearly concerned about this possibility; for example, he has attacked Poilievre throughout the leadership, with tweets accusing Poilievre of "lying" about opposing vaccine mandates "from day one" and the like.[17] For the 5 percent gain on the Far Right, however, the Tories risk losing a far greater number of centre-right voters who look askance at the fringe elements the PPC has attracted.

Which brings us to the state of Canadian conservative politics, circa 2022. While the influence of populism is not new, its latest incarnation feels that way thanks to its similarities to the recent American Republican experience under Donald Trump. In terms of substance, Bernier's PPC builds on the anti-immigration fervour Trump generated in the early stages of his government in 2016. In terms of style, Poilievre's campaign and tactics hew heavily to those of Trump: the absence of Conservative branding, the use of big rallies, simple phrases, and the demonization of elites and of the media. Both leaders also draw similar crowds to Trump: mostly white, lower and middle income, and heavily concentrated in exurban and rural milieus.

Poilievre also styles himself in the mold of a more agreeable, and Canadian, populist: a young Preston Manning. Poilievre sports similar glasses and an earnest demeanour. He engages in folksy banter and says "God bless you" a lot; many of his events have the feel of an evangelical revival. Poilievre also lectures, reaching back into history to tell his audience about "King John and the Magna Carta," or explaining that the House of Commons is green because it represents the common people, who tilled the green fields. He rails against the gatekeepers for holding back the people just as Manning railed against Ottawa for holding back the West.

The 2022 version of populism also comes with something less savoury: a heavy dose of conspiracy theory. In a piece for the *Globe and Mail*, journalist Ian Brown spends time with a host of people who attended the convoy protests.[18] All of them subscribed to various conspiracy theories, from suspicion of the World Economic Forum (WEF) to a recent story that "confirmed" that Justin Trudeau owns shares in a British Columbia–based company connected to Pfizer's COVID vaccine. Brown notes that there is no evidence this is true. Neither is there any evidence for another theory he encountered—that Google calls its search engine "Chrome" and its navigational software "Adrena" to dog-whistle the word *adrenochrome*, a substance which, according to QAnon, is being harvested from the pineal glands of kidnapped children to confer everlasting life to Satanists, including Justin Trudeau.

If you think politicians would avoid going down such bizarre rabbit holes, you are sadly mistaken. Several of the candidates in the leadership race have leaned into conspiracy theories. Social conservative candidate Leslyn Lewis has openly courted supporters who believe that the World Health Organization (WHO) is plotting to gain control of Canada's pandemic response by means of a "global pandemic treaty." Lewis "exposed" what she claims are "people with connections to the Trudeau Foundation and the WHO were deliberately trying to silence me," including Dr. Kelley Lee, who raised Lewis's suspicions because her work is funded by the Canada Research Chairs Program, which is funded by the federal government and overseen in part by the Canadian Institutes of Health Research, which reports to the health minister, who is, "of course," a Liberal (this, Lewis found suspicious).[19] In an email to CPC members entitled "Victory at the World Health Assembly!"[20] Lewis writes, "We won!"—claiming partial credit for changes to the WHO's amendments on pandemic response and pledging to "never back down from a fight with the WHO, WHA, WEF, or any organization that wants to infringe on our sovereignty."

Another candidate appealing to the conspiracy crowd is Roman Baber, whose anti-lockdown stance got him ejected from the Ontario Progressive Conservative caucus when he was an MPP.[21] Baber has expressed opposition to vaccines, tweeting comments such as, "Public health and the "experts" are blaming Delta instead of admitting they were wrong or worse, they lied about the longevity of the vaccine. We were told the vaccine was our ticket out but six months later we need a booster? Why trust public health?"[22]

Not to be outdone, Poilievre has jumped aboard the anti-WEF bandwagon, tweeting that as prime minister he would ban his ministers from attending the annual event in Davos. He has also advanced

a conspiracy theory about the WEF and housing prices: "The globalist World Economic Forum—which Trudeau, Freeland, and Carney so
adore—says, 'You'll own nothing. And you'll be happy.' Maybe that's
why government is inflating home prices."[23] In early June, Poilievre
introduced a private members' bill to ban all vaccine mandates, tweeting
that "the COVID control freaks are never satisfied. Now they want to
push to mandate a third dose."[24]

Poilievre was also taken to task for using the phrase "Anglo-
Saxon" in an interview with writer-philosopher Jordan Peterson. The
phrase is considered a dog-whistle to white supremacists and the
"Great Replacement" theory that posits that immigration is designed
to "replace" the Anglo-Saxon (white) race in Western countries. This
conspiracy theory has been advanced by American extremist Marjorie
Taylor Greene as well as by Pat King, one of the organizers of the Freedom Convoy.

While Poilievre has openly rejected the theory, he and other
Conservatives remain associated in much of the public mind with the
convoy and the conspiracies attached to it. This is problematic for two
reasons. The first is that these theories should not be given the time of day
by the Conservative Party or any legitimate political party. The second
is that, as previous chapters have discussed, the Conservatives have an
image problem when it comes to racism and intolerance. Anything that
reinforces this perception, true or not, risks resurrecting these tropes
and tarnishing the Conservative brand. It gives the Liberals an opening to paint the Tories as Trumpian, conspiratorial, fringe, and the like.
And even if the next leader of the party succeeds in bringing forward a
centre-right, big-tent platform, such associations could lead to charges
of a "hidden agenda" and torpedo the effort.

In other words, association with the Convoy, and Convoy conservatism, could be political poison among the broader electorate. But that
doesn't mean that a populist wouldn't use Convoy Conservatives to win
the leadership—and then change his or her tune once the general election rolls around.

Could this be the end game? In 2006, Poilievre said these words to
national political writer Paul Wells:

"This is the interesting story of Stephen Harper. Everyone thinks he seduced the centre. It's actually the way he tamed the Right . . . He's now taken the most left-wing position of any conservative party in the world on gay marriage . . . [he] has ruled out any abortion legislation. He has basically moved the party onto an agenda that is centrist and acceptable to mainstream people. And he's done it almost without a peep from the right—from the people who founded the Reform Party, who had made the bombastic and even embarrassing remarks that had come to typify the Reform era. All of those people have gone along with this swift, centrist move while making almost no sounds at all."[25]

Could the next Tory leader woo and tame the populists in 2022 just like Harper did with social conservatives in 2006? Could he or she bring them into the tent under the pretext of doing their bidding, while planning to take the party to the centre right after all?

If so, they had better watch out. Previous experiments in the leaderships of 2016 and 2020 showed the folly of running for leader as one thing and prime minister as another. Both Andrew Scheer and Erin O'Toole were demonized by elements of their party for such hypocrisy, with O'Toole in particular pilloried for morphing from "true blue" to a more crimson-tinged shade of blue.

An alternative would be for the next leader to throw the populist flank a couple of meaningless bones in an attempt to keep them happy. In a piece published April 29, 2022,[26] Wells asks this very question, citing Poilievre's pledge to audit the Bank of Canada. Wells equates this promise with some of the moves Harper made to please his Quebec base, including getting the province a seat at UNESCO. It received a lot of fanfare but made little difference in the day-to-day lives of Quebecers. Wells concludes,

"If some issue is important to a faction in a complex party, one option is to embrace the discontent and then propose what are, in the end, nearly insignificant responses. To be rhetorically hot and procedurally cool. A danger, of course, is that you'll be a kind of sorcerer's apprentice, whipping up extremism. But it's also possible that, simply by lending an ear to some widespread concerns . . . you might even have a positive influence."

While I agree with Wells's analysis in principle, I am not sure that it would end on a positive note. As mentioned above, the Convoy constituency contains some elements who might not be easily tamed. While there are many people within it who are simply legitimately angry with the direction Trudeau has taken the country, there are also fringe elements who have shown their willingness to go to the mat for their convictions, even if they end up in prison.

It is also unclear what will happen to the Conservative Party if it pulls in thousands of new members who aren't actually conservative—or even politically engaged. While attracting new blood is crucial for the party to grow, a wholesale transfusion may not be in the party's interest. A movement is not a party—Reform learned this the hard way. Members who come for the show mean little; you need to make those people into worker bees before and during the next election. They need to be willing—and interested—in putting their shoulder to the wheel for all the mundane tasks: literature drops, canvassing, lawn signs, getting out the vote, social engagement, and recruiting their friends and neighbours to the task. You want new members who are willing to be political in the partisan sense of the word. And you also can't afford to alienate existing members who are up to doing that grunt work, because if they sit on their hands during the next election, you lose a large part of your machine—and your ability to get out your vote.

Where would populism take the Conservative Party in 2022? Would it attract a new generation of voters, or fizzle when vaccine mandates are no longer an issue? Would it broaden the tent to bring in more working-class supporters, or become a Trump-like cult of personality? Could it even be called the Conservative Party if people who join don't consider themselves conservative?

The party will decide by September 10. Members also have three other candidates to choose from: Jean Charest, Patrick Brown, and Scott Aitchison. All three eschew the populist label and tack to the centre right. Charest would likely remake the party in the image of the former Progressive Conservative Party. He espouses fiscal conservatism, is pro-choice, explicitly rejects American populism, and is a robust defender of national unity. He proposes to champion national projects such as resource development and military bases in the North, would reform health care, and would grow the party in Quebec.

Brampton mayor Brown is similarly described as a progressive conservative. He has taken a hard-line stance against Quebec's Bill 21, which bans public servants from wearing face coverings and religious symbols. Brown has aggressively courted New Canadian communities with a promise to protect religious liberty, but also made other less well-known promises to various immigrant groups, including offering an apology to the Tamil community, improving cricket infrastructure, and putting a visa office in Kathmandu.[27]

Rounding out the field is centre-right candidate Scott Aitchison, the MP for Muskoka. Aitchison has styled himself as a peacemaker, calling for civility in a contest that has had precious little so far. Aitchison has also gone to war on supply management, the cartel-like system that guarantees price stability to dairy and poultry farmers but excludes new entrants to the market and raises prices substantially for consumers. Opposing supply management was the same hill Maxime Bernier chose to die on in the 2017 CPC leadership race—in part because it whipped up his support in Alberta. While the policy flies in the face of market principles and is analogous to that which underpinned the Canadian Wheat Board that Harper dismantled in 2011,[28] the chief reason Aitchison appears to have championed it is to wedge Poilievre's PPC-based support after Bernier slammed Poilievre as "leftist" on the issue.[29]

While candidates work to out-wedge each other, play the fear factor, or blanket social media with posts of "My crowd is bigger than your crowd," the real ballot question in this leadership remains the same: which man or woman represents the party's greatest hope of winning the next election? To answer that, we also need to answer another question: does the path to victory lie through populism, conservatism, or a combination of both?

We've examined Canadian populism; now it's time to take a deeper dive into Canadian conservatism. What makes a Canadian conservative? And how could the party draw on its conservative heritage to attract the Common Sense voters necessary for victory?

CHAPTER FIVE

CONSERVATISM IN CANADA:
BUILDING THE BIG TENT

On April 11, 2022, Evan Solomon, host of CTV's *Power Play*, decided to stage a debate between a representative each from the Jean Charest and Pierre Poilievre camps. He invited me in my role as national co-chair for Charest's campaign, and Jenni Byrne, senior advisor to Poilievre and former advisor to Stephen Harper. What followed was a no-holds-barred conversation about the leadership race, the candidates, and the state of the party.

Several times, Byrne implied that Charest and I were not true Conservatives, "having just joined the party a couple of months ago." Never mind that Charest had been a minister and leader of the Progressive Conservatives, one of the parties that became the Conservative Party, and that I also had been active for fifteen years in that party and had written about the conservative movement ever since. In Byrne's view, we failed the purity test: Progressive Conservatives like us were not true Conservatives.

The vision presented by Byrne assumes the Conservative Party arose in a vacuum, with nothing before it, no history. As we know from the previous chapter, that is manifestly not the case. The Conservative Party has been through many iterations, including those shaped by populist forces. The party can trace core conservative principles back through time. Those principles are crucial to maintaining its appeal to both current and future members. The essence of conservatism is that it looks to the past for guidance. It seeks to conserve the good of what came before, including political heritage.

The Convoy Conservatives, however, are not seeking to conserve. In fact, the moniker may be a misnomer: they don't even use the term "conservative" at all. I witnessed this firsthand, at a rally the Poilievre team held at the Steam Whistle Brewery in Toronto on April 19, 2022. Poilievre spoke for over half an hour to a rapt crowd of close to a thousand people and did not say the word once. The loudest cheers he received were for three policies that are hot buttons for specific groups of voters: defunding the CBC, promoting Bitcoin, and eliminating vaccine mandates. Not exactly a traditional conservative manifesto.

To be fair, Poilievre also hits on issues of concern to a wide swath of the electorate: the cost of living, the difficulty in buying a home, and challenges for immigrants to gain a foothold in the economy. But his prescription for these problems is not conservative but populist. Poilievre's oft-repeated exhortation to "remove the gatekeepers" is a classic populist stance.. This anti-elitist rhetoric is not about lifting people up but about tearing another group down. It feeds a blame game that creates an us-versus-them mentality, even within the party Poilievre wants to lead.

Which got me thinking—what would be a conservative response to these issues? How do Canadian Conservatives define themselves? Who do they think belongs in their party? And how can the Conservative Party hold together with these populist tensions—or can it at all? Can populist and conservative thinkers live together in one big tent? Or will this rift herald yet another breakup of the party and again keep the Liberals in power for a dozen or more years?

Let's look at the language currently in use in this debate. The Convoy Conservatives' raison d'être can be summed up in one word: freedom. Its fans claim that freedom is the common element that unites different types of conservatives. While this may sound simple in theory, in practice it is riddled with contradictions. Social conservatives may want freedom to worship God "in their own way," but they also seek to restrict women's freedom to have an abortion. Progressive Conservatives believe that people should be free from discrimination but require the state to restrain the freedom of those who would discriminate against others (such as businesses who would not hire minorities or LGBTQ2S+ individuals). Convoy Conservatives want freedom in their personal medical choices but at the cost of the freedom of the citizens of Ottawa to live peaceably in their own city. And at the cost of the freedom—and lives—of persons vulnerable to COVID due to age and pre-existing conditions.

Poilievre said this at a rally in Vancouver on April 8, 2022: "Freedom is a contract between the dead, the living, and the yet to be born . . . It may be eight hundred years old, but it is only one generation deep."[1] Sounds profound. But those aren't his words. He cribbed them from the founder of conservatism, British philosopher Edmund Burke, who in 1790 declared that "[Society] is a partnership in all science, a partnership in all art, a partnership in every virtue and in all perfection. As the ends of such a partnership cannot be obtained in many generations, it becomes a partnership not only between those who are living but between those who are living, those who are dead, and those who are to be born."[2]

Burke's meaning is very different. He spoke of the intergenerational bonds of society, while French Enlightenment philosopher Jean-Jacques Rousseau spoke of the "social contract" between rulers and the ruled, a completely separate concept. In his seminal work *How to be a Conservative*, British philosopher Sir Roger Scruton observes that "[Society's] binding principle is not a contract but something more akin to love. Society is a shared inheritance for the sake of which we learn to circumscribe our demands, to see our own place in things as part of a continuous chain of giving and receiving, and to recognize that the good things we inherit are not ours to spoil."[3]

And yes, contrary to one of British Conservative prime minister Margaret Thatcher's most misinterpreted quotes, Conservatives do believe in the existence of "society." What Thatcher actually meant when she said that "there is no such thing as society" was not that it does not exist, Scruton writes, but that it is not synonymous with the state.[4] Similarly, Burke was in favour of local civil society over top-down government, but he still believed that society must constrain certain individual freedoms for the benefit of the group as a whole.

Burke's vision of freedom is antipodal to that of Rousseau and the Convoy. "Of all the loose terms in the world, liberty is the most indefinite," writes Burke. "It is not solitary, unconnected, individual, selfish liberty, as if every man was to regulate the whole of his conduct by his own will. The liberty I mean is social freedom. It is that state of things in which liberty is secured by the equality of restraint. A constitution of things in which the liberty of no one man, and no body of men, and no number of men, can find means to trespass on the liberty of any person, or any description of persons, in the society. This kind of liberty is, indeed, but another name for justice; ascertained by wise laws, and secured by well-constructed institutions."[5]

Burke's philosophy is rooted in law and order, not "the will of the people." It is also hierarchical, incremental, and opposed to revolution. Burke decried the excesses of the French Revolution and was a fierce critic of the naked rationalism of the Enlightenment. Rousseau, by contrast, was a hero of the revolution, championing a populist uprising; he was also revered in America by its revolutionary founders.

The division between Burke and Rousseau is one of the distinctions that separates British and Canadian conservatism from the American version. As Canadian conservative philosopher George Grant observed, "The founders of the United States took their thought from the eighteenth-century Enlightenment. Their rallying cry was "freedom." There was no place in their cry for the organic conservatism that predated the age of progress. Indeed, the United States is the only society on earth that has no traditions from before the age of progress. Their right wing and left wing are just different species of liberalism."[6]

Grant also saw "progress," as embodied in America's love affair with technological advancement, as anathema to conservatism. (One can only imagine what he would have to say about Bitcoin.) He concluded that "the impossibility of conservatism in our era is the impossibility of Canada. As Canadians we attempted a ridiculous task in trying to build a conservative nation in the age of progress, on a continent we share with the most dynamic nation on earth. The current of modern history was against us."[7]

Grant despaired that Canada would be ultimately subsumed into the United States through a combination of economic and cultural integration. Despite deep ties between the two countries, including two free-trade agreements, this has not happened—yet. If anything, Canadian and American attitudes on a host of metrics have diverged over the years. Canada is a far more liberal country on many fronts, as is evident in its championing of abortion access and the rights of the LGBTQ2S+ communities. It is also a more statist country, with a government health-care monopoly, higher taxes, more regulation, and state interventionism. It is far less religious than the United States; a full 32 percent of Canadians identify themselves as agnostic, atheist, or non-religious, compared to 19 percent of Americans.[8] Canadians also report being less patriotic, career-focused, and materialistic than their southern neighbours.[9]

The greatest difference between the two countries, however, is that, in addition to the First Nations living here, Canada has not one but two founding peoples. Over time, the tension between Canada's "Two Solitudes"—Anglophones and Francophones—led to the development of a federalist–separatist axis rather than a left-right axis. National unity has arguably played the greatest role in the evolution of Canadian conservatism and its divergence from the American version. The challenge of keeping the country together created three things: a culture of brokerage politics and compromise, which tempered political extremes; an expansion of the federal government as a defender of Canadian federalism, which entrenched a more statist worldview; and a diversion of political resources to the cause of national unity, which delayed the evolution of conservatism in Canada compared to its counterpart south of the border.

I explored these ideas with my co-author Adam Daifallah in *Rescuing Canada's Right*.[10] We documented how the struggle to keep Canada united in the face of Quebec's separatist forces resulted in Pierre Elliott Trudeau's government channelling "vast amounts of public money and resources into a massive infrastructure of statist organisations that reinforced his vision of Canada"[11] in the 1970s. We concluded that, "the Liberals succeeded in equating statism with Canadian nationalism, and Canadian nationalism with the big-government policies of the Liberal Party. The Conservative Party failed to challenge these policies and still fails to challenge them for fear of being called un-Canadian."[12]

This does not mean that Conservatives cannot challenge this vision, and indeed, after we wrote those words in 2005, the Harper government did just that. But until then, throughout the 1980s and 1990s, the battle over Quebec separation dominated the political conversation at the same time that American conservatives were debating how to reduce the role and size of the state. Through the Meech Lake Accord, the Charlottetown Accord, and the 1995 Quebec referendum, Progressive Conservative prime minister Brian Mulroney and subsequent leader Jean Charest devoted significant energy and time to keeping the country united. While both worked to shrink the federal deficit and implement market-oriented conservative policies, such as the Canada–US Free Trade Agreement, they also had to spend significant political capital just to keep the country together.

There are only so many hours in the day. While Reform beat the anti-deficit drum in the 1990s, and the federal Tories voted in favour of a 10 percent tax cut at their 1996 policy convention, neither party formed government for over a decade. Instead, it was Liberal prime minister Jean Chrétien and his finance minister, later leader, Paul Martin who slayed the Canadian deficit in the late 1990s, faced with an ultimatum from the IMF.[13]

In 2006, Stephen Harper's Conservative government came to power and held it until 2015. During that time, it took the party further right, embracing the conservative ideas of balanced budgets, lower taxes, and a smaller state. When the deficit-reduction project was derailed by the Great Recession of 2008, Harper took the pragmatic path, returning to red ink and government bailouts in an attempt to avoid a collapse of the housing market and other key industries. Nonetheless, the commitment to smaller government had become more clearly etched in the party's DNA.

During this same time, the separatist threat in Quebec began to wane. Today, the movement is weaker than ever: while the Coalition Avenir Québec made headlines for recruiting former Parti Québécois cabinet minister Bernard Drainville to its ranks in the spring of 2022,[14] the PQ is practically on the verge of extinction.[15]

You would think the national unity issue would now be in the rear-view mirror but it is not. Instead, it has shifted from one end of the country to the other, and once again represents a challenge not only for the country but for Conservatives.

Today, the greatest threat to national unity lies in the West. The demonization of the oil-and-gas sector by both the Trudeau government and the environmental movement, the economic downturn caused by years of low petroleum prices, and anti-vaccination sentiment in Western provinces have all contributed to a feeling of alienation from the rest of the country, a sense that the West is not getting a fair shake and is being held back. Oil prices may be up due the conflict in Ukraine, but the effects of the last recession still linger.

Thus, even today, Canadian prime ministers and Canadian federal political parties have to contend with the unity issue. That involves regional, linguistic, and cultural compromise. Over time, our culture of compromise has meant that successful Conservative leaders have not had to veer as far right as their American counterparts on social or economic issues, instead hewing to the centre right.

Progressive Conservative stalwart and erstwhile "happy warrior" Hugh Segal has written extensively on the subject. Segal views traditional conservatism as "a balance between enterprise and social responsibility, between personal freedom and social obligation."[16] To this end, he quotes British conservative philosopher Michael Oakeshott:

"Now, the disposition to be conservative in respect of politics reflects a quite different view of the activity of governing. The man of this disposition understands it to be the business of a government not to inflame passion and give it new objects to feed upon but to inject into the activities of already too passionate men an ingredient of moderation; to restrain, to deflate, to pacify and to reconcile; not to stoke fires of desire but to damp them down. And all this, not because passion is vice and moderation virtue but because moderation is indispensable if passionate men are to escape being locked into an encounter of mutual frustration."[17]

The great Canadian Conservative leaders have always understood this. Macdonald did, Mulroney did, and Harper did as well. They were able to build big tents and win big majorities by tempering extremes, not playing to them. All three understood that governing is a balancing act. Each had their own challenge: Macdonald's was nation-building, Mulroney's was nation-keeping, and Harper's was nation-changing. While none accomplished everything they set out to do, they each engaged in the project with honour and enthusiasm and have gone down in history as a result.

In contrast, the populist cry of "freedom" is anything but moderate or conservative. It is not about respecting individual rights and collective responsibilities equally but about disregarding responsibilities in favour of rights. It echoes Grant's observation that, "[Americans'] concentration on freedom from governmental interference was more to do with nineteenth-century liberalism than with traditional conservatism, which asserts the right of the community to restrain freedom in the name of the common good."[18]

Freedom is a central tenet of conservatism, but it is traditionally counterbalanced with responsibility. The Conservative Party's constitution cites as its first principle, "A belief in a balance between fiscal responsibility, compassionate social policy that empowers the less fortunate by promotion [sic] self-reliance and equality of opportunity, and the rights and responsibilities of individuals, families, and free associations."[19] It is this recognition that rights and responsibilities go hand in hand that is central to Canadian conservatism. One is not meant to exist without the other.

While Grant feared that economic and cultural integration would pave the way for an American takeover of Canada, the current rise of populism actually creates the greatest risk of assimilation, by transforming Canadian politics into a mirror of the American experience. Charest rightly describes it as the "Americanization" of Canadian politics.

Beyond the polarization, hostility, and tribalism, the true Americanization lies in the abandonment of the Canadian conservative principles of moderation, community, and civic duty. But it is on those very principles that Conservatives can return to power, rebuild a big tent, and regain a majority government—thanks, ironically, to a decision by none other than Justin Trudeau.

CHAPTER SIX

OPPORTUNITY KNOCKS! WILL CONSERVATIVES ANSWER?

On March 22, 2022, Prime Minister Justin Trudeau dropped a bomb-shell. "Today, I am announcing that the Liberal Party has reached an agreement with the New Democratic Party to deliver results for Canadians now. This supply-and-confidence agreement [1] starts today and will be in place until the end of this Parliament in 2025. What this means is that during this uncertain time, the government can function with predictability and stability, present and implement budgets, and get things done for Canadians."

After a pause for dramatic effect, Trudeau intoned, "It was not an easy decision. With so much instability around us, Canadians need stability." [2]

It was a master stroke—or so it seemed at the time. Trudeau's call for stability was a direct response not only to the chaos of the convoy but to the opposition of the Conservatives to the invocation of the Emergencies Act. It was also a counterpoint to the call for "freedom" that had antagonized Liberals, Club Conservatives, and Common Sense Canadians alike.

But it may not have quite worked out the way Trudeau planned.

Within hours, Conservative leadership camps started getting calls from prominent Blue Liberals who were shocked and angered by the deal. For many, this was the last straw from a prime minister who they already held in disrepute. Just as many Red Tories had been dismayed by MPs supporting the convoy, Blue Liberals felt equally betrayed by their leader's "friends with benefits" deal with the NDP.

That sentiment appears to be growing. In an address to the C.D. Howe Institute June 1, former finance minister Bill Morneau lamented his experience in the Trudeau cabinet. "I struggled to get our government to focus on the need for sustained economic growth because it was constantly crowded out by other things that seemed more politically urgent . . . Even if they weren't truly as important." Conservative strategist Mitch Heimpel reflected on this and the Ontario Liberals' rout in the 2022 election (where they did not reclaim party status) and concluded that a shift is happening in the Liberal Party that is leaving "business Liberals" out in the cold[3]—or as Charest called them in the first leaders' debate, "political orphans."[4]

So should the Conservatives open a Blue Liberal foster home? Sign the adoption papers? This may already quietly be happening. Back in the Tory fold, the Liberal–NDP deal inspired the creation of a group calling themselves "Centre Ice Conservatives"—a collection of centrist politicos ranging from Red Tories to Blue Liberals. Contacted when the story of their emergence broke in April 2022,[5] founder Rick Peterson said that "he expected maybe ten or eleven people to join" but within days, had seventy-five people reach out to him. After the English-language debate in Edmonton on May 11, in which candidate Pierre Poilievre promised to fire the governor of the Bank of Canada, Peterson reported that they had an uptick in interest, and that hasn't stopped since. "We've had a huge interest in both media and political circles in what we're doing and our views on the CPC leadership race. Our advisory council list includes people like Marjory LeBreton, Dominic Cardy, Laurie Hawn, Rick Anderson, and continues to grow as well." What is the goal of the group? "Simply to become a powerful and thoughtful voice for mainstream Canadians. We've been able to do that very well so far during the leadership race, not showing favouritism to any one particular candidate but offering support for ideas and views from several of them, and that will continue."[6]

It is clear that there is now a political vacuum on the centre right that the Conservatives are primed to fill—if they pick the right leader, the right policies, and the right path. A path that appeals to the Common Sense Canadian voter not just of today but tomorrow. One that addresses critical issues not with slogans but actions. A path that leads to the goal Common Sense Canadians crave most: not a nihilistic concept of freedom but the tangible promise of opportunity.

What is the difference? A uniquely pro-freedom agenda ignores the fact that in a democratic society, freedom is never absolute. As Burke plainly stated, "The liberty I mean is social freedom. It is that state of things in which liberty is secured by the equality of restraint." In other words, my freedom ends where yours begins. Government's role is to mediate and enforce the compromises that citizens arrive at through the exercise of their democratic rights. This includes the creation of regulation, the passage of legislation, and the establishment of judicial and law enforcement institutions that ensure that laws and regulations are respected.

Freedom to protest is also not absolute. Freedom of expression and freedom of assembly are protected by the Charter of Rights and Freedoms, and on occasion the exercise of those rights may interfere with the exercise of other people's rights and freedoms. That interference, however, must be proportional; since the advent of the charter in 1982, it has been subject to "reasonable limits prescribed by law." An example would be a protest that snarls traffic on a Sunday afternoon, which would likely be considered proportional. Should that same protest snarl traffic for a week or more and cause a large number of people to lose their freedom to work, move about, and peaceably enjoy their neighbourhood, that would likely be considered disproportional.

The Convoy disregarded this proportionality principle. Protesters angry about a number of issues, including vaccine mandates, but more broadly, the Trudeau government itself, occupied downtown Ottawa for three weeks. A number of businesses were forced to close due to the actions of the protesters; local workers lost wages as a result. There were multiple reports of people being harassed for wearing masks, as well as women and visible minorities being singled out for abuse. A female nursing student living in downtown Ottawa told *NBC News*, "They're targeting anyone who's wearing a mask, anyone who's respecting public health policy. I myself have been accosted at least three times. I had one man try to rip my mask off. I've been screamed at, I've been told to go back to my country."[7]

Residents in the affected area were unable to sleep as horns blared day and night until an injunction was granted. The protest morphed into an occupation and spawned additional protests at three border crossings with the United States. These caused an estimated $6 billion in losses and constituted an international embarrassment, doing untold damage to Canada's reputation as a stable, peaceable place to do business.[8]

The protesters unfortunately also did untold damage to the word "freedom" as a rallying cry for Conservatives. Instead of equating it with Ronald Reagan calling, "Mr. Gorbachev, tear down that wall!" or Brian Mulroney calling for freedom from apartheid for South Africa, Canadians now visualize the convoy. And what do they think of it? A poll done by EKOS Research in May[9] found that 63 percent of Canadians opposed the convoy movement, while 23 percent supported it. The balance of 12 percent neither supported nor opposed it. When broken down by party, 90 percent of Liberal voters and 83 percent of NDP supporters opposed the convoy; 5 percent and 7 percent supported it, with the balance neither supporting nor opposing. Among CPC voters, 46 percent supported the convoy, 30 percent were opposed, and 21 percent neither supported nor opposed it. Among PPC voters, those numbers were 76 percent in favour, 18 percent neither supporting nor opposing, and 4 percent opposed.

Conservatives thus have a choice. They can run a populist election campaign on freedom, which will attract a substantial portion of CPC and PPC voters but also alienate an overwhelming number of potential Blue Liberal switch voters. They will not grow their base, and they will not win a general election. They will associate their party with a term that has become toxic in the minds of many voters, just as they were tagged with the "racist" tag following the Barbaric Cultural Practices snitch line of 2015. They risk carrying this association forward into the future and being haunted by it in future elections for years to come.

Alternatively, Conservatives could reject the tarnished cry of "freedom," and campaign on a positive conservative term that all Canadians can embrace: opportunity. The opportunity to own a home, to find a job, to get an education. The opportunity to have a better life for oneself and one's children.

Opportunity depends on more than just freedom. It depends on structures that support those goals: a strong health system, a good school system, a fiscal framework that fosters entrepreneurship and does not penalize hard work through overtaxation. The opportunity to secure a fulfilling, well-paying job depends on the interplay between industry, government, and civil society groups; major projects no longer move ahead without social licence, whether from Indigenous communities or local ratepayers' associations. The opportunity to forge one's path in life—to have a family, meaningful work, community engagement, and the faith of one's choosing—all depend on both freedom and restraint, in the form of social rules people agree to respect in order to live in harmony with each other.

Opportunity depends on both the individual and the collective. It is not the preserve of the Far Right. It is not the rallying cry of the Convoy. It is the true term that unites Conservatives across the spectrum, without the stigma now associated with the word "freedom."

Opportunity conservatism is not new. Back in 2005, in *Rescuing Canada's Right*, Daifallah and I described the concept thus: "Opportunity conservatives frame the role of the state, and every policy it implements, through the lens of creating opportunity."[10] Recently, the president of the Macdonald–Laurier Institute, Brian Lee Crowley, called on the Tories to run on a "hope, growth, and opportunity" agenda in the next election.[11] Crowley identifies a number of policy areas where such an agenda would not only benefit the party electorally but would benefit the country— including Indigenous reconciliation. "A pro-opportunity Conservative Party that embraced Indigenous Canada as a respected, necessary, and welcome partner in unlocking prosperity would find a growing audience in the Indigenous world. And they'd have the foundation of that distinctive Tory narrative on social issues that Canadians seek."[12]

The term "Opportunity conservatism" has also popped up in the

American Right, as far back as 1983, when Republican congressman Newt Gingrich formed the "Conservative Opportunity Society," a group that both influenced Reagan's presidency and paved the way for the Republican Party's 1994 "Contract with America." The conservative think tank The Heritage Foundation discussed the concept of "opportunity conservatism" in 2013;[13] the same year, Republican presidential candidate Ted Cruz said, "So let me suggest an alternative course: opportunity conservatism. Republicans should conceptualize and articulate every domestic policy with a single-minded focus on easing the ascent up the economic ladder. [14] Author Heath Mayo proposed the same in 2018 as a blueprint for post-Trump recovery.[15]

Access to opportunity depends directly on that ascent up the economic ladder, otherwise known as social mobility. However, not everyone is able to grasp the brass ring in equal measure. Doors are closed to some by virtue of skin colour, gender, or lack of education; they open to others by virtue of family connections, wealth, or advanced degrees. The result is inequality. Inequality has long been assumed to be the root cause of populism: the greater the disparity between the haves and have-nots, the theory goes, the more likely populist movements will spring up. Increasing gaps between the rich and poor, rising CEO salaries, and growing concentration of wealth have all been traditionally cited as fomenting populism.

This assumption has recently been challenged, however, by research showing that it is the *type* of inequality—not inequality itself—that fuels populist fervour. It is when the inequality results from unfairness that people get upset. In a paper released in 2019, Harvard scholar Eric Protzer argues that populism is fuelled by a sense of economic unfairness—and that the antidote is policies that promote equality of opportunity, not result.[16] People do not resent *fair, unequal outcomes* where everyone has the same opportunity to take their shot, regardless of social standing or personal characteristics. What they resent are *unfair, unequal outcomes*, where advantage is conferred by privilege regardless of merit, as well as *unfair equal outcomes*, where advantage is conferred by identity regardless of merit.

The first—unfair, unequal outcomes—are the product of oligarchy and elitism, which favour those with connections (your parent is an alumnus, so as a "legacy" you get into an Ivy League school regardless of your grades).

The second—unfair equal outcomes—are the result of government intervention based on membership in an identified group (you are a member of a visible minority, so you get into the same school on the basis of a racial quota).According to Protzer, "Humans do not simply care about the magnitudes of final outcomes such as losses or inequalities. They care deeply about whether each individual's economic outcomes occur for fair reasons. Thus citizens turn to populism when they do not get the economic opportunities and outcomes they think they fairly deserve."[17]

Together with Paul Summerville, adjunct professor at the University of Victoria, Protzer went on to co-author a landmark work, *Reclaiming Populism: How Economic Fairness Can Win Back Disenchanted Voters.* In it, the authors present empirical evidence that low social mobility—the inability to better one's station—correlates with a rise in populism, both within and across developed countries. It is not the fact that young people cannot afford a house that makes them embrace populism. It is the sense that they did everything right—got a degree, a job, saved for a down payment—and still cannot buy that house. It is the sense that they deserve the opportunity but that something—or someone—is depriving them of a fair shot.

When too much of this unfairness builds up, societies are more likely to embrace populism as the solution to their problems. This is why Poilievre's "gatekeepers" argument finds traction in conversations on housing, cost of living, and vaccine mandates. It is the easy fix: blame the elites for your problems. Remove them, and all will be well. This populist solution, however, ignores the fact that it is not the elites *per se* who are the problem but the lack of equal opportunity for others to challenge the elites' hegemony. Unless you address the second issue, you will not change the dynamic but simply replace one set of elites with another.

Joel Kotkin, the American urbanist, takes a similar view. Kotkin paints a picture of a "political volcano," describing how the 2022 French election illustrated the increasing polarization of the votes of the disenchanted middle class. This phenomenon is not limited to Western democracies, however. "This growing class division is a global phenomenon," Kotkin writes. "In 1974, the proportion of global corporate income that went to labour was about 64 percent. It dropped to 59 percent by 2012. This pattern has applied not only to wealthy markets in the West but also to labour-rich markets like China, India, and Mexico."[18] Kotkin notes that in 2017, the Pew Research Center found that poll respondents in France, Britain, Spain, Italy, and Germany were even more pessimistic about the next generation than those in the United States. Youth in Japan and India felt the same way.

Kotkin concludes, "This erosion of opportunity sets the stage for a potential combustion of class anger, particularly as the pandemic and now Russia's invasion threaten to make things worse. The unemployment rate reached 32.5 percent in South Africa during the pandemic years, with almost two-thirds of young people having no job in sight. The story is unfortunately similar elsewhere in Africa, with regional powers such as Kenya and Senegal reporting over 40 percent unemployment. This is a recipe for chaos. Several Latin American, African, and Middle Eastern countries have also defaulted on long-term loans, and more may follow."[19]

In the early phase of the pandemic, Canada had yet to experience a populist wave. At the time, Protzer and Summerville singled out our nation as an example of a country where twenty-first-century populism had failed to catch fire. "In Canada," they write, "the populist People's Party totally failed to connect with any salient issue in the 2019 federal election and received less than 2 percent of the national vote."[20]

Since then, however, things have changed. The combination of Trudeau's big-state solutions and embrace of woke culture, together with the geographic, generational, and worker-class divides caused by the pandemic, have created a sense of economic unfairness. The first sign of trouble manifested itself during the 2021 federal election. The election was notable not simply for the growth in the PPC, which doubled its share of the popular vote to 5 percent, but for the rise of violence on the campaign trail. On one occasion, the prime minister was pelted with gravel at a campaign stop; at another, he had to cancel an event entirely.

There were also over a hundred incidents of violence against poll workers, many related to mask-wearing.[21]

The second sign was the Freedom Convoy and the ensuant 2022 Conservative leadership race. The convoy channelled the expression of that unfairness and was supported by many in the Conservative Party, including the leader, many MPs, candidates for the party leadership, and rank-and-file members. However, as we saw in the polling cited above, its goals were not supported in the same measure by the population at large, nor by the accessible "Blue Liberal" voter pool among Common Sense Canadians that Conservatives need to win over to win the next election.

The result is that today, in 2022, Canadians are deluged by headlines about populism. The division does not lie in the population as a whole, however, but on the right side of the voter spectrum. Just as Social Credit rose to prominence, just as the Reform Party claimed official opposition, a large number of Conservatives are embracing populist solutions to social problems. And just as in decades past, this threatens to split the right-of-centre vote and allow the Liberals to take and keep power.

To avoid this outcome, Conservatives need to address populism—but not embrace it. This means acknowledging its causes and advocating for policies that will address inequalities and *defuse* tensions rather than increase them and inflame them. It means resisting the temptation for simple solutions that may be short-term vote-getters—but have long-term consequences for the fate of the party.

And they may not be vote-getters after all. Summerville predicts that populism in Canada will subside as a movement as the pandemic recedes, yet another reason for the Conservative Party to avoid heading down the populist road. Interviewed on *The Agenda* with Steve Paikin, Summerville compared Canada's experience to that of Sweden, where the migrant crisis of 2016 produced a short-lived populist wave that failed to establish a sustained political movement once the crisis had waned.

"Our argument would be what's going on in Canada is a very natural expression of political discontent after a two-year pandemic,"

Summerville stated. "There's a very specific group of people who are anti-vax, who are anti-mandate, have certain grudges against government, but our argument would be that once the blockades are dismantled, that this will fade as a memory in Canada. We're not going to see some political realignment that's going to create the kind of political disruption, institutional disruption that we've seen in the United States and in the UK.[22]

Should the Liberal–NDP deal hold, the next election will be almost three years away, putting the pandemic even further in the rearview mirror. Nonetheless, economic uncertainty and the cost of living will remain a factor. Should social mobility decline—or even be seen to be declining—due to adverse economic events, populism could remain a political force. Research has shown that the mere perception of increasing inequality can fuel populism,[23] even if it is not borne out by the facts.

In a thesis published in 2019, researcher Laura Brogi correlated the perception of lack of social mobility with the propensity of Italians to vote for the populist Northern League Party (Lega Nord). Even though voters were not experiencing actual social stagnation, the perception that they were due to "import shocks" from China, which had caused job losses and the export of manufacturing jobs, was sufficient to fuel the populist flame.[24] The League capitalized on this "perception is reality" phenomenon, similar to how populist politicians in Canada are capitalizing on the wave of reports of economic shocks from inflation.

So what is the solution for the Conservative Party? It is not about being "Liberal-lite," as Tory leader Candice Bergen decries.[25] It is about appealing to Common Sense Canadians on the basis of Canadian conservative values, not aping their American populist counterparts. It is not by chanting "freedom," pledging to defund the CBC, making it easier to use Bitcoin, and promising to make Canada "the freest country on Earth" that Common Sense Canadian voters will be won over. Canada already ranks sixth in the world in terms of freedoms, according to the Human Freedom Index, co-published by the Cato Institute, the Fraser Institute, and the Liberal Institute at the Friedrich Naumann Foundation for Freedom,[26] none of which are left-leaning institutions. Voters aren't looking for a high school civics lesson on liberty. They are looking for a better life for themselves and for their children.

Protzer and Summerville are very clear: the solution lies in creating a society that favours fair unequal outcomes and equal opportunity. There is no single set of policy prescriptions for this, but they do depend in part on the state. "In an entirely laissez-faire society, disparities in parental wealth mean that some naturally gifted citizens will not be able to afford education, private transport, or housing in city centres, and can be bankrupted by an unexpected layoff or illness,"[27] the authors observe. At the same time, they stress that society must not "punitively cut down the most prosperous members of society and transfer wealth from the rich to the poor *en masse* for the sake of equalization itself."[28] Instead, society should embrace value creation through an efficient market economy, and punish rather than reward "cheaters" who attempt to get ahead at the expense of others.

Conservatism is founded on the principle of equality of opportunity, not result. Burke articulated it thusly, "Whatever each man can separately do, without trespassing upon others, he has a right to do for himself; and he has a right to a fair portion of all, which society, with all its combinations of skill and force, can do in his favour. In this partnership all men have equal rights; but not to equal things.[29]

Conservatism is neither redistributionist, nor elitist. It does not seek to remake society but rather ensures that all have a fair shot at achieving their dreams. It relies on a strong justice system to ensure all citizens are treated fairly and equally. It cherishes democratic institutions. It values law and order and does not kowtow to mob rule. It values freedom of speech but balances that freedom—like all freedoms—against the interest of the community and its "little platoons."

Conservatives need to craft policies that respect these values. The best antidote to economic populism remains social mobility, and the best means of ensuring social mobility is to ensure equality of opportunity, not result. Rather than fuel class conflict by obsessing over gatekeepers, Conservatives should unify Canadians by creating gateways to opportunity.

It is now up to the Conservatives to channel that spirit into their policies to win the next election, and the ones after that. Conservatives need to convince Common Sense Canadians that they are on their side, that they are not beholden to region, class, or prejudice, and that they stand up for the unity of the country. And they need to do it in the places they are weak: among New Canadians, in cities and suburbia, among young people, and in Quebec. Unless they expand in those markets, they will not win. It is simple math. So let's now examine what those practices and policies could be.

CHAPTER SEVEN

IMMIGRATION NATION:
THE NEW CANADIAN VOTE

It's a truism that Canada is a country of immigrants. Since Jacques Cartier first planted a cross on the banks of the St. Lawrence in 1534 and claimed all he could see for the King of France, successive waves of migrants have sought new opportunities on our shores. After the initial mix of French and British settlers, the 1800s saw the arrival of American colonists seeking land grants, Irish refugees fleeing famine, Chinese workers building the Canadian Pacific Railway, and Japanese migrants seeking better economic prospects. In the 1900s, Eastern Europeans sought out the Prairies, while a wave of Europeans and Britons followed in the aftermath of World War II. Since 1970, migrants from India, Asia, South Asia, and Africa compose the bulk of new arrivals. Currently, just over one in five Canadians was born somewhere else; by 2036, that number is predicted to rise to three in ten.[1]

In 2022, the case for immigration boils down to simple demographics. Canadian women have one of the lowest replacement fertility rates in the Western world: 1.5 children as of 2018. (By comparison, the US replacement fertility rate is 1.7; in Mexico, it's 2.1, which is the minimum number that ensures each set of parents replaces themselves with another generation). Fewer babies today mean fewer workers down the road. Current immigration goals are thus based on meeting the needs of the labour market. The government's 2022–2024 Immigration Levels

Plan sets a target of 1 percent of Canada's population, equal to a growth of 431,645 permanent residents in 2022, 447,055 in 2023, and 451,000 in 2024.[2] Many business leaders have also signed on to the Century Initiative, which seeks to increase Canada's population to one hundred million by the year 2100.[3]

This need for immigration presents a philosophical challenge for the Conservative Party. It is difficult for a country built by wave upon wave of immigration to be "conservative" in the literal sense of the word. Conservatives look to the past for guidance; perpetual immigration begets perpetual change, particularly when newcomers come from different backgrounds, cultural norms, and worldviews. Even in a melting pot like America, it is difficult to leave behind all the beliefs with which one was raised. In a mosaic like Canada, where newcomers are encouraged to maintain their cultural identity, it is even harder to "conserve" a consistent national character.

Elements of the Canadian character have come into question, particularly in the last six decades. Starting in the 1960s, state-funded multiculturalism policies began diluting the "two founding peoples" concept of the Canadian nation. The brainchild of Liberal prime minister Pierre Elliot Trudeau, the federal government's goal was to counter the threat to national unity posed by separatist forces in Quebec; the side benefit was to ingratiate the Liberal Party with every ethnic and cultural community, as they were then known, in the country. The result was the creation of a "third solitude" known as "allophones" in Quebec (persons whose first language was neither French nor English), and "ethnic" in the rest of Canada.

In more recent times, the decolonization movement has attacked the foundations and architects of the modern Canadian state. Statues of Conservative prime minister John A. Macdonald, the father of Confederation, lie beheaded on the pavement. Ryerson University has been renamed Toronto Metropolitan University in light of reports of mass graves of children at former residential school sites in Canada, and there are calls for McGill University to change its moniker as well, given the fact that James McGill owned slaves. Social movements including #MeToo and Black Lives Matter have fuelled demands for atonement and institutional change.

Canada's government and its historical figures have no doubt committed their share of sins and atrocities in the past centuries, for which they should make amends. However, it is equally important not to erase national achievements that have produced the country we inhabit today. The reason many immigrants came to Canada is that it presented a land of opportunity superior to that which they left behind. Atoning for mistakes must be counterbalanced by a sense of gratitude for what we have inherited: a democratic, peaceable nation with a high standard of living, freedoms enshrined in and protected by law, and a culture that supports individuals in the attainment of their dreams.

As Brian Lee Crowley, President of the MacDonald Laurier Institute, puts it, "This gratitude for our inheritance is in contrast to the Left's obsession with our mistakes, our moral, environmental, and racial failings, for example. The past is no source of inspiration but is composed of endless sins whose stain can be removed only by endless apologizing, the abandonment of tradition, and the reconstruction of our institutions and behaviours in accordance with fashionable opinion."[4]

As described in the earlier chapter on wokeism, populist movements thrive in such an environment. When historical narratives are challenged, citizens who identify with them feel assailed as well, and may seek to "reclaim" the symbols of what they feel they have lost. The trajectory of the Canadian flag illustrates this narrative arc. In the past twenty years, the flag has morphed from a symbol of Canadian pride, sewn onto the backpack of every Europe-bound university student, to a symbol of shame, lowered to half mast over the discovery of mass graves at the site of former residential schools, to a symbol of populist discontent, waving from the backs of pickup trucks and the sides of the eighteen-wheelers that occupied Ottawa during the Freedom Convoy.

What does the flag mean now? That depends on your perspective. In February, the *Globe and Mail* published a series of letters about the use of the Canadian flag at the Freedom Convoy. Responses varied. One letter-writer said, "I settled in Canada as a young refugee from East Africa. The Canadian flag to me has meant fealty to tolerance and respect." One writer felt that "the Canadian flag still represents our great country, but now I feel it represents something more: a movement of people who've had enough of lockdowns, mandates, and job losses over a medical choice." Another lamented that "with all the turmoil in our country, I don't know what it means to fly the Canadian flag anymore."[5]

The impact of this polarization and confusion cannot be understated. Nations are constructed around facts, myths, and symbols, designed to inspire national pride and a shared sense of purpose. Without those, the tie of common citizenship is severed. Conservatives recognize this; as British philosopher Roger Scruton puts it, "We don't require everyone to have the same faith, to leave the same kind of family life, or to participate in the same festivals. But we have a shared civic culture, a shared language, and a shared public sphere . . . Over time, immigrants can come to share these things with us . . . And they more easily do so when they recognize that, in any meaningful sense of the word, our culture is also a multi-culture, incorporating elements absorbed in ancient times from all around the Mediterranean Basin and in modern times from the adventures of European traders and explorers across the world"[6] (and in the case of Canada, from Indigenous Peoples as well).

The impact of polarization is particularly toxic for newcomers who are not yet fully integrated into Canadian society. What are New Canadians to think about the country they have chosen to make their home? Is it, as the woke would say, an oppressive colonialist regime, bent on upholding a white capitalist patriarchy while keeping down Indigenous people as well as visible and sexual minorities? Or is it, as the populists would say, a government-dominated society serving only woke elites to the detriment of hard-working, tax-paying "regular people" who have had it with political correctness?

The reality is that neither is correct. Both left-woke and right-populist extremes perpetuate these stereotypes for their own purposes, which are to reshape society in their image and serve their own interests. It's not about getting rid of "oppressors" or "gatekeepers," but about installing the ones they favour.

Neither extreme serves the interest of the Common Sense Canadian. They also do not serve the electoral purposes of the Conservative Party. The first demonizes Conservatives as defenders of a legacy of oppression. The second depicts Conservatives as victims of woke politics.

Who would want to join a party filled with people like that?

The chief beneficiary of this state of affairs is the Conservatives' natural foil: the Liberal Party. Over the past fifty years, the Liberal Party has staked the claim as "the party of immigration."This is ironic when you consider that the first leader of the federal Conservatives (yes, Macdonald) was an immigrant, and the first prime minister not of English or French descent was a Progressive Conservative (John Diefenbaker, of German heritage). It is even more ironic when you consider that the Liberal Party has perpetually been led by native-born members of the Laurentian Elite, including our current prime minister who has blithely sported blackface at home, and Indian wedding outfits abroad.

In identifying—and being identified—as the party of immigration, the Liberals have an advantage over the Conservatives: they aren't likely to be tagged as intolerant. In contrast, the Conservatives routinely fall prey to this label. The recent history of the party has not helped. Neither has ignorance of what it has achieved in the past.

In the 1980's, it was the Progressive Conservatives, not the Liberals, who championed immigration. According to former prime minister Brian Mulroney, "When I came in, the Trudeau government had brought in sixty to seventy thousand [migrants] a year—by time I left, that had increased to three hundred thousand, the highest number in Canadian history [to that point]."[7]

Mulroney went on to note that his government indicated to multiple constituencies that the Progressive Conservatives were interested in their welfare and would defend their interests. "We put through the Japanese redress and apologies, an apology to the Italian community, we set up a Nazi war crimes commission," he added. Under Mulroney's watch, Lincoln Alexander was appointed the first Black lieutenant governor of Ontario, and Yvon Dumont, the first Métis lieutenant governor of Manitoba, becoming the first Black and Métis persons, respectively, to serve in a vice-regal position in Canada.

So, what went wrong? According to Mulroney, the Reform Party. "Reform was seen as xenophobic and anti-gay. Manning and Harper should be ashamed for themselves for what they ran on in 1993. They destroyed the PC party. And what did we get? Nothing—but we gave

Jean Chrétien thirteen years in power. Reform destroyed a lot of the goodwill of the PC part of the ledger for immigrants. It drove them away from the Conservatives, even under the united party."[8]

People also seem not to know that Harper's Conservatives admitted more immigrants to Canada than Jean Chrétien's Liberals had[9]; what they remember is the proposed "barbaric cultural practices" snitch line and Harper's foot-dragging on the admission of Syrian refugees. This has deterred New Canadians from feeling at home with Conservatives and supporting their cause. It also does not help that right-of-centre parties are identified, not only in Canada but around the world, with anti-immigration policies. Here at home, it is not the Conservatives but the People's Party of Canada that claims that dubious status—yet the tag sticks to the Tories anyway.

So what are the bases for making conservatism—the worldview, the philosophy, the vision—relevant to New Canadians? It is allowing them to identify with it as a gateway to opportunity and to see themselves in its future. To do this, the party has to both talk the talk, and walk the walk.

First, the walking. Today's Conservative Party is not diverse. Its elected membership is akin to a 1950s golf club: male, older, and white. Only seven of the 119 Conservatives elected in 119 ridings are Black, Indigenous, or people of colour (BIPOC)—which works out to only 6 percent of the current Conservative caucus.[10] That is down from 9 percent in the past election. In contrast, the Liberal caucus is 30 percent BIPOC. And despite the negative experiences of former Liberal MPs as Jody Wilson-Raybould and Celina Caesar-Chavannes, the Liberals can still legitimately claim to more accurately represent the diversity of our country.

That must change - but how? Let's take a second look at those community-minded businesses with considerably lower stakes: private golf clubs. The golf clubs that have survived—and even thrived—have expanded their membership, attracting women and non-white players to their ranks. But why would an immigrant join the Conservative Party? What would its appeal be? It's a vicious circle: unless there is something to attract New Canadians, the party will remain that of Harper's "old-stock" Canadians;[11] unless New Canadians can see themselves in the party, they will be less likely to join.

That *something* is the talking. If Conservatives present an inclusive and appealing message, it will not only attract New Canadians but also reinvigorate the party's base. It will create a common bond between new and old, as opposed to emphasizing or exploiting division.

The key is to reconcile conservative values with the solutions to people's problems. For New Canadians, the problems to be solved are those of establishing themselves in a country often very different from the one they left. Finding work, building a home, raising their children, and—as any child of immigrants will tell you, possibly the most important thing—enabling those children to do better than their parents.

As a daughter of immigrants, I vividly recall the aspirations— and expectations—of my parents, who came to Canada penniless in the 1960s. My mother's family had lost everything for having resisted the Nazis in Germany during World War II. My father decided to move to Canada following the death of his first wife in the Middle East, where he had fled after deserting the German army during the war. Canada welcomed them, but they had to work long and hard to make their way. They sacrificed to send me to private school—no family vacations, new clothes, or new cars. In return, I was expected to bring home straight As. I recall once hiding my report card in shame when I placed third instead of first. I recall feeling different from my classmates, whose mothers did not give them liver sausage sandwiches for lunch or shop at thrift stores. I also recall that my fierce desire to be successful and make my place in the world was bolstered by my wish to not let my family down.

My own early ambition correlates with the experience and outcomes of children who came to Canada as immigrants versus children born in the general population. In 2018, 70 percent of twenty-year-old immigrants who were admitted to Canada before the age of fifteen participated in post-secondary education, compared to 56 percent of the overall population of twenty-year-olds in the same year. Thirty-two percent of those immigrant post-secondary students lived in low-income households, compared to 15 percent of their non-immigrant peers. They also went on to out-earn those peers: at the age of thirty, native-born Canadians reported a median wage of $41,810, compared with $47,400 for thirty-year-old immigrants admitted as children—a 13 percent difference.[12]

How do the values of conservatism and the Conservative Party relate to this type of immigrant experience? In the 2022 leadership race, candidates are courting New Canadians in a variety of ways. Pierre Poilievre is emphasizing freedom, which, for immigrants who come from countries that are manifestly unfree, such as China or Iran, can be immensely appealing. On its own, though, freedom is not enough. For example, my parents knew what communism was—they despised it in all its forms—and they staunchly believed in freedom. Yet they voted Liberal for most of their lives; Pierre Elliot Trudeau had liberalized divorce laws (which had allowed them to get married, since my mother was in an unhappy union when they met!), and he then brought in the Charter of Rights and Freedoms. Consequently, they never felt that Conservatives had a monopoly on the term "freedom." For today's newcomers, Conservatives need to realize that the gulf between our government and those of unfree nations is so wide that even the Liberals may appear to offer sufficient freedom for their purposes.

Furthermore, as already discussed, the term freedom has become tainted by its association with the Freedom Convoy. And for many New Canadians, particularly of visible minority or religious background, that has particular significance.

Walied Soliman is the Canadian chair of Norton Rose Fulbright, a top international law firm, and has been involved in conservative politics since the age of fourteen. A practicing Muslim, Soliman has been instrumental in bringing Muslim Canadians into the Conservative fold. Soliman is also a childhood friend of Patrick Brown and one of Brown's key advisors and organizers. When asked what New Canadians think of when they hear the word *freedom* in the mouths of Convoy Conservatives, he shakes his head.

"They hear freedom to troll me on the Internet, unchecked; they hear freedom to swear at me in a mall because I'm wearing a headscarf; they hear freedom to protest outside my place of worship. They hear freedom to do all the things that make their lives worse."[13]

What New Canadians crave more than anything, Soliman says, is not freedom but security. "Immigrants come here from places where they were insecure, where they were persecuted for their beliefs. They couldn't plan a future for themselves or their children. Their top need is personal security, to live their lives in peace and see their kids thrive. Since 2015, Conservatives have not made New Canadians feel that a vote for us will give them secure lives as human beings."

One of the young Conservatives I spoke with expressed a similar concern. Arjun immigrated to Canada at the age of three from India, and grew up in the GTA, mostly in Brampton. Now twenty-two, he recently graduated with a degree in political science, and is considering a career path in law or politics. He has always "leaned right," but for a time the niqab ban gave him pause. "For many young people it comes down to very important questions about relevant things to them, like housing affordability, the cost of living, and work. Historically, a lot of young people always felt that the Conservative Party has a very good way to deal with these issues, but there were a number of policies that a lot of young people probably were not as in favour of. The niqab ban was one of these policies that definitely alienated me as a young person from wanting to get involved in the Conservative Party."[14]

According to Soliman, it's not the number of people directly affected, but the message sent to the broader community that was the problem. "The number of women who wear the niqab in Canada is maybe two hundred. I don't know a single person who does. But when we came out with the niqab ban, it was an attack on the security to wear and worship what you choose. The thought process goes like this: that can be extended to the hijab, to whether you can pray at your mosque, to whether you can pray at all. That means I may not be secure in this country under a Conservative government. And that's when immigrants stop listening to us, and start listening to the Liberals."

The irony is that Conservatives have much to say to New Canadians, if they can get them to listen. One of the main points of connection is faith. Edmund Burke considered religion to be one of the pillars of conservatism, and the Church one of its "little platoons." He was appalled by the French Revolution's attack on the Catholic Church and staunchly defended religious liberty, attacking the anti-Catholic laws the English imposed on Ireland and speaking in favour of the 1772 Toleration Bill, an act that proposed to grant freedom of worship to "nonconformists" such as Protestants and Congregationalists. Burke stated that "the very principle of toleration is that you will tolerate not those who agree with you in opinion, but those whose religious notions are totally different."[15]

Burke not only displayed respect for—but also interest in— non-Christian religions such as Hinduism and Islam. In a letter written in 1775 he stated, "I would give a full civil protection, in which I include an immunity, from all disturbance of their public, religious worship, and a power of teaching in schools, as well as Temples, to Jews, Mahometans, and even Pagans."[16] He contrasted the attitudes of the "tyrannical" British East India Company with the rule of Islamic states, where clerics had the "moral authority" to check the excesses of princes.

These religions are on the rise in Canada due to immigration. By the year 2036, the number of people affiliated with non-Christian faiths could almost double, to make up between 13 percent and 16 percent of Canada's population, compared with 9 percent in 2011. In contrast, according to a report by the Church's statistics and research officer, the Anglican Church will run out of members by 2040.[17]

Immigrants consider religion a more important part of their life than native-born Canadians. Among all persons born between 1980 and 1999, those born outside Canada were much more likely than those born in Canada to report a religious affiliation (71 percent versus 59 percent) or to consider their religious beliefs to be somewhat or very important (62 percent compared with 39 percent). In comparison, those born outside Canada between 1940 and 1959 were about as likely as their Canadian-born counterparts to report a religious affiliation (85 percent versus 87 percent) and only slightly more likely to consider their religious beliefs to be somewhat or very important (74 percent compared with 66 percent).

Burke viewed religion as a counterweight to the power of the state. He also recognized the power of ritual, tradition, and "the sacred," which he believed elevates humanity and gives life meaning. Conservatives would not demand that an individual choose between church and state in the exercise of their employment. Several leadership candidates, including Brown, Leslyn Lewis, and Roman Baber, have thus actively opposed Quebec's Bill 21, which denies public servants the right to wear any type of religious symbol while on the job. Conservatives should defend religious liberty at home and abroad, and call out prejudice based on faith.

The second pillar Conservatives share with New Canadians is family. For Conservatives, it constitutes another crucial counterweight to the state, and perhaps the most important "little platoon" of all. It is no accident that in communist countries, there have been attempts to dismantle the family. Government overreach is only possible if there are no other sources of support to turn to, and the family is on the front lines.

Here, the Conservatives need to first repair some of the mistakes of the Harper government with respect to immigration policy. The big one was the prioritization of economics over compassion, notably by reducing family-class immigration. Parents and grandparents could no longer apply for sponsorship to immigrate—they were permitted only to visit under the terms of a new "super visa" as long as their families could pay for health care and other costs.[18] The visa allowed for multiple re-entry points for a total of ten years' visiting, but was valid for only two years at a time. That had a personal, immediate, and negative impact on millions of New Canadians who could no longer have their extended families join them in a sustained and predictable way.

Going forward, Conservatives would be well advised to stop viewing family reunification as a drain on resources and to embrace it instead. This is consistent with the conservative view that the family is the basis for society and that organizations exist to strengthen its bonds. Individuals should be free to make choices toward their own self-realization while enjoying the support of their community. Many immigrants seek to bring extended family to Canada, including parents, not simply because they are close on a personal level but also because their family can help in caring for children. There are more intergenerational households among New Canadians than among the native-born. Parents and grandparents are caregivers, yes, but they also act as a means of passing culture on to the next generation. That demands more than a two year window.

The Liberals have already twigged to this. In June 2022, they extended the "super visa" aimed at parents and grandparents of citizens and permanent residents to seven years as opposed to two. "Families are at the heart of Canadian society," said immigration minister Sean Fraser. "The enhancements to the super visa program allow family members to reunite for longer in Canada, which helps everyday Canadian citizens and permanent residents succeed and contribute to society, while affording their parents and grandparents invaluable opportunities to spend time with their family in Canada."[19]

Conservatives need to similarly emphasize family-friendly policies. These include policies that make having and raising children more affordable and flexible. Both Charest and Lewis are advocating policies to extend parental leave to two years in order to increase the time parents can spend with their children. Lewis's plan would also start paying benefits in the twelfth week of pregnancy to allow expectant mothers to feel less pressured to work in the later stages of pregnancy. As it is now, many expectant mothers continue to work right up until their babies are born. Charest, Lewis, and other candidates also support increased childcare options for parents to ensure parental agency.

Lewis would also bring back family income tax–splitting for spouses, introduced under the Harper government but then rolled back by the Liberals after the 2015 election. If the Conservatives were to focus on appealing to families with children, they could expand on this by introducing income-splitting between parents and children as well, as is the case in France.[20] This would appeal to all families but would be particularly attractive to larger families, which, when compared to native-born Canadians, immigrants statistically tend to have.[21]

The third pillar of conservatism is free enterprise, which refers not only to entrepreneurs but also to the ability of persons to be able to work in a profession or job of their choosing without barriers imposed by the state in the form of regulation. Chief among these are credentials requirements of professional governing bodies, as are enforced by the medical profession or skilled trades. A long-standing complaint of New Canadians is that their credentials earned outside the country often remain unrecognized here in Canada, thereby preventing them from working in their field of expertise. This is an issue that Conservatives should champion and that has already featured prominently in the platforms of several candidates including Poilievre, Brown, and Charest.

Beyond credentials, however, is the greater issue of establishing connections necessary to professional advancement. Mentorship projects, skills workshops, and political engagement workshops are all activities that Conservatives should engage in to connect with New Canadians, establish relationships, and be of value. Politics is as much a social exercise as it is an ideological one, and forming personal connections is a powerful way to open the door to potential support and civic engagement.

These efforts, however, should not be taken on solely out of MPs' offices. Apart from increasing office workload, immigration outreach demands a level of understanding of community relationships that may be beyond that of constituency staff. A more effective model is for the Conservative Party would be to deploy specialized field organizers whose sole responsibility is to connect with community leaders and build bridges with the party. These field organizers would then be able to ensure that when MPs engage with diverse groups, they are properly briefed and do not make unforced errors such as "taking sides" with one group or another who may represent different points of view within the same community. This strategy was used in Quebec during the Mulroney years and worked well to build support with the allophone groups of the day, including the Greek community.

Finally, while Conservatives should make every effort to attract New Canadians to their party, they must remain mindful of geopolitics and national security concerns. CSIS has documented increasing foreign interference in Canadian elections, and we are seeing an increase in disinformation by state actors such as China.[22] This was in evidence in the 2021 federal election.

In 2021, the Conservative platform included several get-tough measures on China, including barring Huawei from 5G networks, implementing Magnitsky-style sanctions on Chinese officials who had been identified as human rights violators, and counselling universities not to partner with Chinese state-owned enterprises. During the forty-third session of Parliament, Tory MP Kenny Chiu advanced a private members' bill, modelled on Australian legislation and similar American provisions, that would have set up a registry for agents of foreign governments.

In the second week of the campaign, Chinese ambassador Cong Peiwu implied that Conservative leader Erin O'Toole preferred to advance the Conservatives' "political interests" over Canada's relationship with China.[23] Suddenly, Chinese-language social media platforms such as WeChat were peppered with lies smearing Conservative candidates, suggesting the party was planning to ban WeChat itself,[24] and websites attacking Conservative candidates Kenny Chiu, Alice Wong, and Bob Saroya sprang up.

Kenny Chiu was targeted originally for his sponsorship of the Foreign Influence Registry Act (FIRA),[25] which would ensure that lobbyists, lawyers, and politicians past and present would need to register as foreign agents when representing the interests of a foreign government. Many current and past politicians oppose this level of transparency, but it is precisely the type of accountability that will help stop foreign interference in municipal, provincial, and federal politics in Canada. America has had similar legislation in place since 1938, and Australia implemented an analogous act on December 10, 2018, after recognizing that many of the country's politicians, academics, and business elites had been influenced or co-opted by Chinese state actors.[26]

According to intelligence sources cited by Sam Cooper, the author of *Wilful Blindness: How a Criminal Network of Narcos, Tycoons and Chinese Communist Party Agents Infiltrated the West*,[27] Chinese interference networks targeted twelve federal ridings. The results surprised the Liberals and the Conservatives alike, and were very disturbing. Disinformation operations linked to groups that had targeted Cooper for reporting on the PPE repatriation to China started amplifying anti-Conservative messages using WeChat. Chiu, who was heavily favoured to win his riding, lost to a no-name Liberal contender. Two other Conservative MPs, Alice Wong, of Richmond Centre, BC, and Bob Saroya, of Markham–Unionville, also lost their seats due to the CCP's United Front disinformation operations. According to Cooper, this was borne out in three separate reports, including one given by the Conservative Party to CSIS that suggested the party was very concerned and "looking for guidance" from Parliament on how to proceed.

The goal of the United Front was to demonstrate its power and influence the vote of the Chinese diaspora community, and its disinformation campaign clearly had the desired effect. Quito Maggi, president and CEO of Mainstreet Research, noticed a shift in the preference of Chinese Canadians early on.[28] Forty-three percent said they'd vote Liberal, while 25 percent picked the Conservatives, and 24 percent backed the NDP. "More than two-thirds . . . supporting non-Conservative candidates was highly unusual," Maggi said. While some observers believe Chinese Canadian voters switched their vote due to anti-Chinese prejudice, or out of personal concern over the Conservatives' stance on China, the size of the swing alone suggests that something else was at play.

Since Kenny Chiu's defeat, Conservative senator Leo Housakos has reintroduced FIRA in the Senate in hopes that Canadians will see it in place by the end of 2022.[29] This would strengthen Canada's ability to work with and negotiate with foreign governments and hold lobbyists accountable, and would help to protect our trade and national security interests. It would also support members of various diasporic communities who are fearful of showing their allegiance to Canada when foreign governments attempt to influence their vote. Defending the sanctity of the right to vote is a policy all parties should heartily defend.

Striking the right balance between growing the Conservative Party, engaging diverse communities, and respecting Canada's interests is a challenge that Conservatives must successfully undertake if they are to expand the tent and win future elections. It should in fact be a lesson to all political parties. If Canada fails to protect its national security through FIRA, enact stiffer penalties for money laundering, as well as increase investment in intelligence and policing to root out spies and organized crime, our democracy will be increasingly vulnerable to attack by hostile nation-states, with potentially devastating consequences.

As the Canadian mosaic continues to evolve, so must the Conservative Party if it is to continue to provide a credible national alternative to the current Liberal government. And as we will see in the next chapter, this evolution is intimately linked to the Conservatives' fortunes in the ridings where they are weakest: urban and suburban Canada.

CHAPTER EIGHT

A COUNTRY OF CITIES:

THE URBAN VOTE

In the 2006 federal election, the Conservative Party engaged in an exercise that has since become standard fare for every political party in the country, and indeed the Western world. It sliced and diced data sets, including postal codes, income levels, and personal characteristics, to identify likely voters. It also identified those who would not vote for it, to avoid wasting resources.

One of these data sets was a voter the Conservatives named "Zoë." Zoë was a single, urban twenty-something female living in downtown Toronto. She rented a condo and ate out in trendy bistros. And she was not likely to vote Conservative.[1]

Jess Goddard is a Zoë. She lives on the Bay Street Corridor in Toronto, near the legislature at Queen's Park. She is twenty-eight, graduated from Queen's University, works for a provincial cabinet minister, and does not own a home or a car. She admits sheepishly that she eats out "a lot." By the Conservatives' definition, she shouldn't be a supporter. And yet, Goddard not only votes Tory but ran as the candidate in Toronto Centre for the Ontario Progressive Conservatives in the 2022 provincial election.

When I ask Goddard why she is a Conservative, the conversation turns to the size of government. "I've seen the way market-driven solutions that used to benefit me as a young person have been made worse by government. When Uber first appeared, sure, it was pretty unregulated, but it was a real answer to how expensive traditional taxis had become—and then the government got involved and barred Uber from Toronto Pearson Airport for no reason. City council added bylaws and made the service less convenient for a higher cost. I also see the amount of taxes taken off every paycheque and I say, okay, what am I really getting for that? Then the government gives away millions of dollars in so-called investments to huge corporations and you think, but that's my money! And those are the same corporations that gouge me every chance they get."[2]

Goddard isn't the only Zoë breaking the mould. Her twenty-seven-year-old campaign manager, Tanu Chopra, is a similar "unlikely voter" according to Conservative archetypes. Chopra came to Canada from Tanzania at age eighteen and decided to stay after attending the University of Toronto. She rents, takes transit, works in finance, and lives in the trendy St. Lawrence Market area of downtown Toronto. She shares some of Goddard's reasons for being a Conservative but not all.

"As a young female, if someone ever asked me my leanings, I would say I would never vote Conservative. I was going to go to a liberal university and was very inclined to believe in ideas on the left. But the anti–free speech movement in universities and [its] takeover at the tail end of my university career in 2016–2017—and then seeing the excess of the Left in the pandemic, given their complete aversion to civil liberties—is what pushed me into thinking like people on the right."[3]

Where Chopra parts company with Goddard, however, is on the issue of government intervention when it comes to workers' rights. She appreciated that the Ontario Progressive Conservative government regulated Uber and other gig economy companies; she had hoped the Liberals would do it and was disappointed when they did not. "I thought, hey, this is what the Left should be doing, but they have completely abandoned it. If the Conservatives will pick up that mantle of fighting for working people, then that's where I find myself."[4]

Has Zoë changed since 2006? The pandemic, woke culture, and economic inequity are all major factors in the lives of young people today; as we will discuss in the next chapter, they may be Conservatives in waiting without knowing it. In 2022, maybe the Conservative Party shouldn't write Zoë off quite so quickly.

Also identified in that 2006 election were three other voter archetypes: "Dougie," "Mike," and "Theresa." Dougie was a tradesman living in rural Nova Scotia; he didn't usually vote, but with the right incentives, like a tax credit for new tools, he might do so. Mike and Theresa were married with three kids; Mike was a salesman and travelled a lot, and between him and Theresa, only one of them had a college education. The couple had left Toronto for the 905 and were likely to vote Conservative. In fact, the Tories learned that they were 50 percent more likely to do so than families with one or two kids, and that for every additional child, the odds of voting Conservative increased.[5] For voters like Mike and Theresa, pocketbook issues tend to dominate the conversation and the election.

Maleeha Shahid knows lots of Dougies, Mikes, and Theresas. She met them as the Conservative candidate in the 2021 election in her 905 riding of Whitby, Ontario, which includes a century-old downtown, subdivisions of townhouses and single-family detached homes, pockets of McMansions, and a rural area to the north. But things have also changed.

"The 905 is very diverse and the Conservative Party has to understand since the election that Stephen Harper lost in 2015 that life and people and their thought process[es] have evolved. Demographics have changed, and until the Conservative Party understands that we have to now be a big-tent party and look at things for the greater good, we're not going to win."[6]

Shahid felt her voters lacked confidence in the party and what it stood—or didn't stand—for. "We cannot have wishy-washy statements or wishy-washy policies. At that time in my election last fall, people wanted to see a mask mandate, people wanted a strong stance on health care. People also wanted to see a strong stance on the fact that this pandemic will be dealt with strong hands."[7]

This time around, what will the issues be? "Running on a strong economy alone does not work. That's not the only thing that constituents are looking for from a federal party. They're looking for climate change action because that does matter to suburban families or urban families. They're looking for jobs and job security but also that the party is inclusive."[8]

So are Mike and Theresa still the Tories' best hope? There is the possibility that they are vanishing due to demographic shifts. For Walied Soliman, that realization hit in 2019 when Tory stalwart and former minister and leadership candidate Lisa Raitt lost her seat in Milton, Ontario. Soliman says it is a direct result of immigration patterns. "All the Muslim friends I grew up with who couldn't afford to buy a house in Mississauga, they bought a house in Milton. It's now out of reach for the Conservatives."

According to Soliman, the Muslim and Sikh vote has eroded since 2015, and with it, the ability of the Conservatives to win the suburbs. If the party continues to align with the Convoy, he fears it may become unattainable. "When people of my generation and my parents' generation see the Convoy, they see crazy people who hate them, and then they see our politicians standing by and supporting them. Then they go on the Internet and see them all doubling down. Milton is just the start. Mississauga might as well be like [the downtown riding of] Trinity–Spadina right now. Milton is out of reach, Mississauga is a lost cause, and Durham Region will be soon too."

Statistics bear out the changing composition of newcomers to areas like Halton Region, which includes Milton, Oakville, Burlington, and Halton Hills in the 905 belt west of Toronto. Prior to 1961, 93 percent of New Canadians came from Europe. In 1996, the balance tipped, with immigrants from Asia and Africa comprising half of all newcomers. By 2016, 70 percent of immigrants hailed from those parts of the globe, while only 13 percent came from Europe, and 14 percent from other parts of the Americas.[9]

These ridings are not only becoming more diverse, but more urban. Mike Ras ran in 2021 in the riding of Mississauga–Lakeshore, a leafy enclave of multimillion-dollar homes and the scenic Port Credit waterfront. The last time a Tory won there was in 2011; since 2015, the Tories haven't won a single one of the six seats in the city of Mississauga, and Ras has a pretty good idea why.

"I think too many of us are still stuck in the belief that ridings like Mississauga–Lakeshore are truly suburban ridings. They are increasingly becoming urban seats. The influx of condos and things like that is certainly a big part of this. We have to be ready for that and find a way of connecting with those voters."[10]

Ras did that in 2021—and lost by only 5 percent of the vote, something he attributes to the fact that the more traditional Tory voters stayed home. "I concentrated on those areas that were gentrifying, that were coming up, where people were moving in, so they were new voters. I overperformed in those neighbourhoods and underperformed in the traditional Tory parts."[11]

Ras thinks the base didn't turn out as much, not because local efforts failed but in part because the central campaign didn't speak to them. "I think people didn't feel that the campaign resonated with them. There was no motivation there. The long-time "duty voters" stayed home."[12] Ras's main takeaway is that the campaign needs to strike the right balance between new and old voters—and not take any archetypes for granted.

The Conservative erosion in urban and suburban Canada is not new. Tories have long lamented their exclusion from big-city ridings, while the Liberals and NDP often take them for granted. This phenomenon can be traced back to the 1920s, but it has not been fully studied until recently.

In 2019, a trio of researchers at Western University, Dave Armstrong, Jack Lucas, and Zack Taylor, published a paper on the rural–urban divide in Canadian politics. They found that a divide first appeared in 1917, following World War II and the emergence of the Progressive Party, but was resolved after that party declined and then disappeared. There was also a brief surge in 1935 due to the popularity of the Social Credit Party, which was concentrated in rural areas.

A durable urban–rural cleavage later emerged among the Progressive Conservative, Liberal, and NDP parties in the early 1960s, was re-invigorated in 1993, and deepened after 2003. These markers coincide with the collapse of Diefenbaker's Progressive Conservative government, ensuant shifts in Canadian immigration patterns, the collapse of the

Progressive Conservative Party, the emergence of the Bloc and Reform Parties, and the creation of the newly merged Conservative Party under Stephen Harper.[13]

While one might assume that this divide would benefit both the Liberals and the NDP, this is not the case. Armstrong, Lucas, and Taylor found that it directly benefited the Liberal Party, and that this "urban advantage" may help explain why, despite the decline of national support for the party, the Liberals managed to dominate the late twentieth and early twenty-first centuries.[14]

Armstrong, Lucas, and Taylor posit that the rise in Liberal fortunes after the 1960s mirror those of the Democratic Party in the United States, which could be linked to the ascent of "urban, well-educated 'knowledge workers' with fiscally conservative and socially progressive attitudes."[15] In Canada, they would likely be called "Red Tories" or "Blue Liberals." This echoes the observations made by Tom Flanagan after the founding of the Reform Party in 1987, about how the Conservatives could no longer depend on the urban middle class, which had become "part of the 'new class,' or 'knowledge class,' as it is sometimes called, and is thus a political class dependent on tax-supported government programs."[16]

And that "new class" has only grown larger with time. The researchers found that by 2019, a one-unit shift in their "urbanity score" for a riding produced an increase of more than eight percentage points in Liberal Party vote share.[17]

Additional insights can be gleaned from the research of Jason Roy, Andrea M.L. Perrella, and Joshua Borden of Wilfrid Laurier and McGill Universities, published in 2015. The trio studied eight provincial election databases for three types of voters—rural, urban, and suburban—and found that each constituted a distinct set. They wanted to know whether their preferences were shaped by where they lived, or by their underlying sociodemographic characteristics.

They found that while suburban residency correlated highly with a propensity to vote Conservative at the provincial level, it varied across the country. "Suburban residency yields a statistically significant increase in the probability of Conservative Party support.—[by 23 percent in

Newfoundland, 21 percent in Manitoba, 20 percent in Ontario, 20 percent in Saskatchewan, and 18 percent in British Columbia] . . . [In] PEI and Quebec, there are no significant effects for either variable." The researchers attributed the results in PEI to population size and lack of ideological difference between provincial Liberal and Conservative parties, and in the case of Quebec, posited that "a combination of the issue of Quebec sovereignty as well as the economically conservative (yet socially centrist) positions of the [Coalition Avenir Québec] may offer some insight into this unexpected result."[18]

In other words, suburban voters in five of the eight provinces examined were more likely than their urban counterparts to support conservative parties. This is important when considering another factor identified by Armstrong, Lucas, and Taylor: seat redistribution. "Enhanced urban representation is not simply the result of urbanization as a generalized national process," they write. "It is also produced by periodic parliamentary redistributions, which have allocated new seats almost entirely to growing urban areas, and large metropolitan centres in particular. It may be no accident that the urbanization of parliamentary representation appears to have increased since Canada adopted independent electoral boundary commissions in the late 1960s. While variation in the population size of districts has favoured rural districts and small provinces, a party with a strong and growing vote-share advantage in urban districts is in a strong position to win elections."[19]

The results of the last election bear this out in the starkest terms. In the 166 ridings made up by the country's three biggest cities, the Liberals won eighty-six, more than half of their national seat total. The Conservatives won just eight. The Liberals won all twenty-five of the most urban ridings in Canada and 109 of the top 150 most urban ridings, while the Conservatives won just twenty-three of those urban ridings.[20]

Politics is linked to economics. Each of the three historical spikes in urbanity's importance to election outcomes corresponds with a period of rapid urban growth and rising urban housing prices.[21] When cross-referenced with immigration data, they also correspond with increased waves of migrants who settled primarily in urban areas, increasing pressure on housing stock and changing the demographic makeup of cities.

In other words, immigration, urbanization, and the entrenchment of the Liberal vote are inextricably linked. These factors are not changing; if anything, they are accelerating as birth rates fall, labour-market shortages persist, immigration levels remain high, and urban areas continue to grow. Suburban areas still provide fertile ground for Conservatives, as measured at the provincial level, but if the federal Conservative Party does not find a way to attract the New Canadian vote, it will fail to recapture these constituencies. If this happens, the outlook is bleak: the Conservatives will eventually become a rural rump party despite their high share of the national vote.

So how do Conservatives recapture the urban and suburban voter? Well, there are specific issues of concern shared by urban and suburban dwellers, regardless of ethnic background. Apart from connecting with the immigrant voter, Conservatives should draw on their principles to address these issues and offer solutions not just to appeal to voters but to provide real leadership for the country.

The first issue is affordability. The cost of housing has been a sore point in urban and suburban markets across the country, most noticeably in greater Toronto and Vancouver. In the wake of the pandemic, smaller municipalities also saw a surge in prices; cities such as Hamilton, Surrey, Halifax, and Fredericton saw prices climb by double digits. As interest rates rise, home values appear to be coming down, but the reality for most urban and suburban dwellers is that unless they have significant savings or a wealthy parent, buying a home in a major metropolitan area remains out of reach.

During the leadership, all candidates have seized on this issue. Poilievre has made home affordability—and affordability in general—the cornerstone of his campaign. "Stop printing money. Build more houses," is one of his recurring themes. One of the means he suggests is having Ottawa influence local zoning decisions by withholding federal infrastructure funds. Other candidates have proposed increasing the housing supply, or offering incentives for purchase through RRSPs and TFSAs.

The reality is that there is no easy solution to high housing prices—and that dropping them also creates a downside. Many voters, particularly baby boomers, are counting on their home equity to fund their retirement.

Many homeowners of all generations are also heavily in debt, having taken out large mortgages or lines of credit that were easy to fund until interest rates started creeping up. A crash in the housing market would send the Canadian economy reeling and shrink the wealth of millions of retirees.

Smart policy should not cause a crash but build a bridge. The underlying issue is not simply the rising price of homes but the gulf between that increase and the increase in wages. Canada has the highest price-to-income ratio of the G7. Salaries have not kept pace with the rising cost of housing. Part of this is fuelled by demand, which in turn is driven by immigration to urban areas. Part is fuelled by speculation and, in the worst case, money laundering, as is the case in Vancouver.[22] The current government has acted on this front, imposing a two-year ban on foreign ownership, but that alone will not solve the problem. And the problem is that the middle class sees their children unable to buy a house in the city where they grew up. This social mobility issue provides fertile ground for populism.

G7 HOUSE PRICE-TO-INCOME RATIO

The indexed value of the house price-to-income ratio for G7 countries, as well as the OECD average.

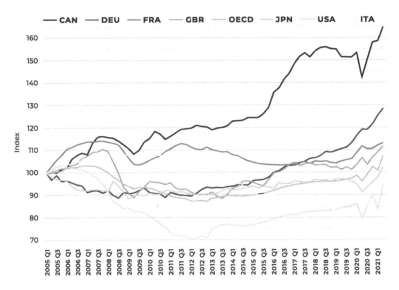

SOURCE: OECD; Better Dwelling

Better Dwellings, December 13, 2021, https://betterdwelling.com/canada-has-the-biggest-gap-between-real-estate-prices-and-incomes-in-the-g7/.

Should Conservatives fan the populist flames to regain the suburban vote? Based on all the research, evidence, and polling, that would be a mistake. As we have seen, populism and the Convoy have become inextricably intertwined in the minds of Canadians. This movement turns off many of the key voters the Conservatives need to attract: suburban immigrants. It stokes the pre-existing racist stereotype that contributed to the Tories' defeat in 2015 thanks to the "barbaric practices snitch line" and revives holdover misgivings about the Right as previously elicited by the Reform Party. It cements the divide between Convoy and Club Conservatives, entrenches the notion that the Conservatives are the party of rural and Western Canada, and leaves Common Sense Canadians out in the cold.

Furthermore, the populist trope of attacking the "gatekeepers" will do nothing to address the underlying issue of affordability. It will not bridge the disconnect between wages and prices. This will require policies that grow the economy, not that demonize the rich. An opportunity-focused agenda similar to Brian Mulroney's "Jobs, jobs, jobs" mantra of 1984 would go further than a "fire the governor of the Bank of Canada" agenda in 2022.

The Conservatives need to increase social mobility without parroting dog-whistle populist rhetoric. Tax cuts that leave more money in voters' pockets is a policy consistent with both conservative principles and increasing affordability. This approach has been adopted by other nations, including the UK, while Alberta has removed sales tax from gasoline. Lowering the gas tax is a no-brainer; Sohaib Shahid, director of economic innovation at the Conference Board of Canada, recommends next removing tax from food, noting, "Low-income households spend 15 percent of their total annual spending on food, whereas high-income households only spend half that."[23]

Conservatives could also incentivize zoning decisions that favour the building of the "missing middle" type of housing that makes cities more affordable. "Missing middle"–type housing is any house-sized dwelling that includes multiple units. Duplexes, fourplexes, courtyard houses, stacked townhomes, granny flats, and laneway housing are all examples of housing options that increase density while keeping neighbourhoods to a more traditional, single-family-home scale. This type of housing is common in Europe. It can be found in abundance in Montreal and other Quebec municipalities but is the exception in cities like Toronto and Vancouver. Conservatives should use carrots, not sticks, to encourage this type of housing, such as additional funds for transit or local projects of importance to urban residents.

With regard to social policy, the most oft-used wedge issue against Conservatives, especially in urban areas and in Quebec, is the issue of abortion. It is a conversation that most do not want to reopen (72 percent of Canadians prefer to keep it closed, according to a Maru poll)[24] but one that the Liberals will raise at the first opportunity to create fear of a Conservative "hidden agenda." The recent leak of a Supreme Court draft decision on the fate of *Roe v. Wade* has once again thrust the issue into the public eye, prompting Prime Minister Justin Trudeau to vow to "protect abortion rights in Canada"[25] without giving more details.

A Leger poll taken shortly after this announcement found that 64 percent of Canadians support introducing a Canadian law to protect the right to abortion. Broken down by party, this includes 74 percent of Liberal supporters, 78 percent of NDP supporters, 51 percent of Conservative supporters, and 84 percent of Bloc Québécois support-ers. Seventy-nine percent support a woman's right to abortion, while 14 percent are opposed.[26] A Maru poll taken during the same time period found 74 percent of Canadians believe a woman should be able to get an abortion "no matter what the reason," while 21 percent believe abortion should be legal only in certain circumstances, and 6 percent say abortion should be illegal in all circumstances; of this group, 66 percent say their religious beliefs inform that view.[27]

To date, the most effective Conservative leader to manage the abortion issue has been Stephen Harper. Harper categorically shut the door on reopening the debate but worked with social conservatives to address other issues of concern, such as defending religious liberty over-seas. In contrast, subsequent leaders Andrew Scheer and Erin O'Toole managed to upset both pro-choice and pro-life voters. Scheer stated he was pro-life but refused to reopen the issue, while O'Toole stated he was pro-choice while defending the rights of doctors to refuse to perform the procedure (and then changing his position). Voters, understandably, didn't trust either of them.

The lesson is clear: Conservatives will not win urban and suburban votes, particularly in Quebec and Ontario, if they take a pro-life position or are ambiguous about reopening the debate. The next leader needs to do what Harper did on abortion: shut the door, lock it, and throw away the key. Social conservatives may not like it, but the alternative is to lose another election and the opportunity to implement any kind of conservative policies at all.

One issue where Conservatives connect well with urban and suburban voters is public safety. On Boxing Day of 2005, during that year's federal election, Jane Creba, a fifteen-year-old high school student, was tragically killed in the crossfire of a gang shootout near Toronto's Eaton Centre. The city was horrified; 2005 had already been dubbed "the year of the gun" due to a record fifty-two homicides that year. According to pollster Darrell Bricker, "That's when the numbers shifted"—in favour of the Conservatives. Harper released a "tough on crime" platform that resonated strongly with suburban voters and brought forward additional measures in the next two elections as well, in 2008 and 2011.[28]

Law and order have always been associated with conservatism; indeed, one of Edmund Burke's most enduring quotations is that "good order is the foundation of all things." One of the difficulties the Conservative Party may face in the next election is squaring that reputation with its support of the convoy protests and its opposition to the use of the federal Emergencies Act, particularly among urban and suburban Red Tory and Liberal switch voters. According to a survey by Angus Reid in May 2022, there is a clear divide among political parties on the use of the Act. Overall, 46 percent of Canadians believe invoking the act was necessary to give police the tools and resources to quell protests, while 34 percent thought the police already had sufficient tools and resources; a further 15 percent thought the protests should have continued with no interference. By party, 79 percent of Liberal voters and 58 percent of New Democrats believed invoking the Act was necessary, compared to only 20 percent of CPC members. Conversely, 27 percent of CPC members believed that the protests should have been allowed to continue with no interference, compared with 1 percent of Liberals and 5 percent of NDP voters.[29]

Another stumbling block to attracting urban voters to the federal Conservative Party is that most other issues of concern to urban residents are not the purview of the federal government. When asked what would excite the voters of Toronto Centre, Goddard did not have an easy answer; apart from general pocketbook issues, transit, and some infrastructure projects, most concerns were local or provincial. Housing, hospitals, schools, roads, and garbage pickup top the list. Chopra observed as well that for well-to-do city residents, it's not money but identity that plays a role in their voting choices. To put it bluntly, they can't see themselves as Conservatives because they associate the party with rural interests or stances on social policies, such as abortion, that they do not share.

But what if one turned this on its head? What if it were made clear to urban and suburban residents that Conservatives were actually the best choice because they believe in the primacy of *local* government? An example would be on firearms policy, an issue that Liberals effectively deployed against the Tories as a wedge in the 2021 election. The Liberals depicted the Conservatives as beholden to the gun lobby, which played against them in suburban and urban areas. But a true conservative position would be to defer to local government on the issue of firearms control. If an urban agglomeration wants different gun regulation than a rural area, so be it. The role of the federal government, when it comes to guns, is solely to prevent illegal guns from coming into the country. While this involves deciding what types of firearms are permitted and which are not, the fact that a municipality could elect to keep certain types out of its boundaries would allow voters to have more control. Municipal elections could even be tied to referenda on the issue, if local legislation were to allow them, giving citizens even more of a say.

Another example where "thinking local" is a Conservative advantage is energy policy. Urban and suburban voters who want action on climate change will look askance at parties that do not offer concrete solutions, including carbon pricing. At the same time, Liberal carbon taxes disproportionately impact rural consumers who have no choice but to use fossil fuels for driving, heating, or operating their businesses. A wheat producer, for example, has to dry his grain with propane. Even before the war in Ukraine caused the price of oil to spike, a farmer in Saskatchewan told me that it would cost him ten thousand dollars just to dry his crop that year. I cannot imagine what it costs now. Energy policy has to reflect these two realities—the urban/suburban and the rural—and attend fairly to both.

The same disproportionate effects resulted from the Liberals' pandemic policies, including CERB and its successor, the Canada Recovery Benefit (CRB), except in this case, urban recipients got the short end of the stick. The CERB amount—two thousand dollars a month—barely covered rent for a studio apartment in downtown Toronto or Vancouver. In many rural areas, however, these payments met or exceeded the local average annual income. According to many small-business owners, it created a disincentive to work that provoked a labour shortage in construction, food services,[30] and agriculture.[31] Part-time workers had little incentive to return to work, with the *National Post* noting that the three-hundred-dollar-a-week CRB benefit "is the amount that a part-time employee working twenty hours a week in Alberta would make."[32] A Conservative version of relief would have accounted for these differences and ensured that recipients got the level of benefits that made sense within their jurisdiction and that businesses did not suffer as a result of overly generous programs.

Policies need to be flexible to recognize the difference between rural, urban, and suburban communities. National, one-size-fits-all policies are not what conservatism is about. Decentralization and local choice are. Conservatives already differentiate themselves from the Liberals on the issue of centralization when it comes to provincial governments, but they should emphasize this on the municipal level as well. "Power to the people" can be achieved through conservative principles without populist demagoguery.

This brings us to a practical issue that Conservatives must address: increasing their representation in municipal government.

Municipal elections in Canada are supposed to be non-partisan; though some cities allow party systems, they are not the same organizations as at the federal or provincial level. It is an open secret, however, that party machines routinely support municipal candidates; the NDP was recently found to have influenced candidate selection in Edmonton's 2021 municipal election.[33] According to a study done in 2020 by Jack Lucas, now associate professor in the Department of Political Science at the University of Calgary, while 30 percent of local politicians described themselves as non-partisan, their views evinced clear leanings toward either a party or political ideology.[34] This puts a lie to previous theories that municipal politics act as a "relief valve" for politicians whose personal politics may not match the leanings of their district, or the "irrelevance" argument that ideology and partisanship don't matter in municipal voting.

Using a national municipal database, Lucas overlayed municipal boundaries with federal polling data to see whether the federal and municipal representatives of each ward or district "matched" in terms of partisanship and ideology. When accounting for party, nearly 40 percent of municipal politicians matched the partisanship of their districts, while 54 percent matched the "ideology" of the party that represented their district. The research did not address the cause of this relationship, but Lucas speculates that personal affinity (i.e., political or ideological alignment between residents and their representative) is the most likely factor.[35]

Municipal election turnout is traditionally the lowest of all levels of government. In Montreal, for example, only 38 percent of eligible voters cast a ballot in 2021;[36] in Calgary, 46 percent did so that same year. Turnout in Vancouver's last municipal election, in 2018, was 39 percent, while in Toronto it was 41 percent.[37] It would therefore be theoretically possible for Conservatives to trump the "natural alignment" found by Lucas if they get behind a single conservative-leaning candidate and focus on their ground game, getting out as much of their vote as possible to support that person. Not splitting the vote is crucial, as is targeting districts where incumbents are not running again, or where the spread between federal Conservative and Liberal candidates in the last election was particularly small.

Focusing energy on local races could transform local government, which in turn could "trickle up" to the provincial and federal level. Developing local talent does two things: first, it provides a farm team of candidates for higher office who have a base of support, a knowledge of their community, and political experience. Second, it makes urban and suburban voters more comfortable and familiar with Conservatives because local voters will already have been exposed to them and their ideas. It builds trust, which is the foundation of any successful political campaign.

Some provincial Conservative parties have already recognized this. In the lead-up to the Ontario provincial election, a series of sitting members of the provincial Progressive Conservative Party decided not to run again. According to a source within his government, Premier Doug Ford actively prioritized the appointment of local elected officials such as school board trustees and councillors as candidates to replace them. Meanwhile, in the current federal leadership race, two of six candidates hail from municipal politics: Scott Aitchison, former mayor of Huntsville, and Patrick Brown, who has run at all levels, but is the current mayor of Brampton.

School boards are another opportunity for Conservatives to become politically active, not only in terms of ease of election (turnout is generally even lower than for city council, so it doesn't take that many voters to win) but that offer the opportunity to expound on an issue of direct concern to Conservatives: the impact of "woke culture" on education. Many parents are concerned about changes to elementary and high school curricula that focus on social justice issues rather than the core ABCs. Others do not agree with the age-appropriateness of content around sex and gender education. This has not gone unnoticed at the federal level; leadership candidate Leslyn Lewis has gone so far as to promise a "parents' bill of rights" should she win the race. But the reality is that activism on these issues is most effective at the local board and provincial level because it can directly impact the delivery of education.

There is no question that Conservatives face an uphill battle to recapture the vote of urban and suburban electoral districts. But unless the party makes headway in these areas, it will not form a majority government. In the lead-up to the next election, anticipated for 2025, the party should build capital in suburbia with New Canadian voters and suburban families. Conservatives should emphasize their bona fides (the economy and public safety) while ensuring that they do not allow the Liberals to wedge them on issues like gun control and abortion. They should offer an opportunity agenda that promises to increase social mobility while eschewing the extremes of populist rhetoric. Niche issues such as plumping for cryptocurrency and defunding the CBC might draw cheers from the base but will do little to expand it. On the ground, Conservatives should field and support candidates in the 2022 fall municipal elections to create as much of a "farm team" as possible for the next federal vote. And as they do this, they should remember that key principle of conservatism: incrementalism. Rome wasn't built in a day, and electoral victories aren't either.

CHAPTER NINE

COURTING YOUNG CANADIANS:

MILLENNIALS AND GEN-Z

Okay, boomer. Your time is up. Ditto for Gen X. Don't take my word for it—take that of the 2021 census.

For the first time since the end of the baby boom, Canadians aged fifty-six to seventy-five make up less than a quarter of the Canadian population, or 9.2 million souls. They represent 24.9 percent of the total population, compared with 41.7 percent in 1966, when their twenty-year-old selves sported bell-bottoms and vowed to never trust anyone over thirty.[1]

Who is taking their place? Millennials, aged twenty-five to forty. They are the fastest-growing generation, increasing by 8.6 percent between 2016 and 2021 to just under eight million people. This increase is not due to births but immigration; over half the newcomers who settled in Canada in those years were millennials. In contrast, baby boomers' numbers are dropping due to deaths—their cohort shrunk by 3.1 percent in the same period—and are past the age where immigration will boost their ranks.[2]

As for Gen X (a name popularized by Canadian writer Douglas Coupland with his 1991 novel *Generation X: Tales for an Accelerated Culture*, kicking off our obsession with assigning letters to generations), they are aged forty-one to fifty-five years and number just over seven million people in Canada, up 2.3 percent from 2016. But that's still small potatoes: Generation Z, aged nine to twenty-four, rose 6.4 percent since 2016 and at 6.7 million, they represent the second-fastest population growth of all generations. If current trends continue, Gen Z could outnumber baby boomers in 2032 and millennials (also known as Gen Y) by 2045.

Millennials now account for the largest share of the working-age population (33.2 percent), constituted of those aged fifteen to sixty-four.[3] They also accounted for more than one-third of the downtown population of large urban centres in Canada in 2021, while baby boomers accounted for one-fifth.[4] By 2029, they will outnumber baby boomers as the largest cohort in the country.

In other words, if the target voter of today is the suburban New Canadian Gen X parent, the target voter of tomorrow is currently an urban immigrant single millennial, and further down the road, their Gen Z equivalents. Unless the Conservative Party can bring these voters into the fold in the long term, it will go the way of the dodo along with the vanishing baby boomer.

So what makes young Canadians tick? Are they potential Conservatives? And how can the party connect with them?

A report published in March 2022 by Environics Analytics, in conjunction with Apathy is Boring, a non-profit, non-partisan group dedicated to increasing youth engagement in politics, takes a deep dive into the lives of millennials and Gen Z and paints a fascinating picture of both generations. "Canadian Youth: A Social Values Perspective—Identity, Life Aspirations, and Engagement of Millennial and Gen Z Canadians"[5] is based on an in-depth online survey administered to over 5,200 Canadians aged eighteen to forty across the country between September 8 and November 9, 2020. The sample was stratified by province, age, and gender according to statistics from the 2016 census. The goal was to see how millennials' and Gen Z's experiences and perspectives are shaped by identities, background, and social values. It should be required reading for whoever wins the leadership of the Conservative Party.

For Canadian youth, personal identity is most strongly linked to their country, gender, and language, and to a lesser extent their generation, religion, and region or province. Almost all identify as female or male; 75 percent consider themselves heterosexual, while one in ten identify as the remainder, naming another sexual identity on the LGBTQ2S+ spectrum. Seven in ten are employed either in full or part time and while most are not satisfied with their current income, most are optimistic about their future prospects. Their highest priority is achieving a work–life balance and financial security. Black youth and South Asian millennials are the most confident in their future careers.

Like those before them, this generation of young Canadians is far from monolithic. They can be classified into distinct groups of social values that include goals, concerns, and political orientation. They are the Dougies, Mikes, and Theresas of Gens Y and Z. The available findings point the way for all parties—including the Conservative Party—on how to engage the voters most likely to be accessible to them.

First, the millennials. The biggest group in this generation are the "bros and Brittanys" (props to these researchers for some very creative names!). Comprising 32 percent of their generation, they are avid risk-takers and enthusiastic consumers. They work hard, embrace technology, prioritize appearance, are not looking to change the world, and don't always feel in control of their destinies. They are more likely to be older, male, and live in Quebec with a partner in a common-law relationship. Ethnically, they are mostly white or Chinese. They have average incomes and close-to-average education. Politically they are centrists, falling on the "average" of the left–right spectrum.

The next largest group are the "diverse strivers," who comprise 20 percent of all millennials. They prioritize "making it," material success, and new experiences. They seek social respect by "doing their duty" and being upstanding members of their families and communities. They are the most multicultural of millennial groups, most likely to be foreign-born and non-white, especially South Asian. They are more likely to be male than female and concentrated in Ontario, mostly in the GTA. They are as likely to be married (though not common law) as other millennials and to have children, despite being younger; those not yet married aspire to having a family. Politically, they are most heavily weighted to the right.

Another group of interest to the Conservatives are the "new traditionalists," who hold values that researchers report would "not be out of place in the 1950s" but who also share twenty-first century concerns— environmental issues, for one. They comprise 11 percent of all millennials. Religion is an important part of their lives and identity. They subscribe to traditional gender and family roles. They cultivate good dress and good manners, respect their elders and authority, report a stronger sense of duty, and identify more with their family roots than their peers. Demographically, they are the oldest of the millennials, more likely to be female, married (but not common law), and have children—but less likely to be employed full time. They have the highest level of education and income of all millennials, in part due to age and matrimonial status. They are overrepresented in Alberta and Manitoba and comprise a high proportion of immigrants, especially those identifying as Black. Politically, they occupy the middle of the spectrum and are the least likely to identify with the Left.

The three other millennial cohorts identified are the "engaged idealists" (17 percent), "critical counterculturalists" (4 percent), and "lone wolves" (16 percent). Politically, none of them identify with the centre or the right; idealists and counterculturalists lean heavily left, while wolves are the least likely to place themselves anywhere on the political spectrum. Ethnically, all three groups identify as mostly white and Canadian-born, though counterculturalists also have a notable proportion of first-generation Canadians.

Idealists are highly educated and remunerated; somewhat ironically, they prioritize meaningful careers over money. They are the most female of the cohorts, likely to live in Ontario and the West with a partner but are less apt to have children.

Counterculturalists are the "quintessential progressives," prioritizing gender equality and diversity, and rejecting any status or authority they deem "superficial." They are by far the most educated group, with one in five having a graduate degree, but they bring in a below-average income. They are most likely to live in BC and be single without children.

Wolves are deeply skeptical of authority. They lack strong emotional and social connections and are rarely connected with whatever is going on in society at large. They are not hostile or angry, however, but low key, and neither xenophobic nor sexist. They are older, found more in Quebec, and if unmarried are uninterested in having children. They are the least likely to be employed full time or to have post-secondary education; they are the most likely to be native-born and white. They tend to earn less than thirty thousand dollars a year.

Based on this research, the Conservatives have a clear "in" with the right-leaning diverse strivers, comprising a total of 20 percent of the millennial population. To get close to the magic 40 percent required for a majority government, the Conservatives need to capture an equal chunk of the remaining electorate as well. The new traditionalists (11 percent) share a lot of conservative values but also care about the environment; unless the Conservatives offer something on that front, they may not be on board. The bros and Brittanys (32 percent) are centrists, which means they are also potentially accessible to the Liberals, unless that party veers too far to the left. The wolves, at 12 percent, are skeptical of authority, which may predispose them to politics that reject over-weening government. However, they may not be easy to motivate; they are not socially engaged and are least likely to place themselves anywhere on the political spectrum.

Now let's look at Gen Z. Among voting-age members of that generation, there are three groups that tilt right: "dutiful accomplishers" (17 percent), "hustling hedonists" (16 percent), and "guarded independents" (12 percent). Together, they comprise 45 percent of the Gen Z population aged eighteen to twenty-four. The first two bear certain similarities to the new traditionalists and diverse strivers and hail more from New Canadian communities, while the last group is similar to the bros and Brittanys but less accepting of difference in identity and perspective on race and gender. Independents are more likely to be white, male, and heterosexual, and to express a greater indifference to violence than their peers.

There are three left-leaning groups among voting-age Gen Z, for a total of 49 percent of that population: the "egalitarian idealists" (26 percent), the "earnest strivers" (15 percent) and the "reflective realists" (8 percent). Ethnically, the idealists are mostly third-generation white Canadians, while the earnest strivers reflect the ethnic breakdown of Gen Z as a whole, and realists have the highest percentage of Indigenous representation.

The only politically centrist group among Gen Z is the "optimistic observers"—at 6 percent. They are also primarily white, third-generation Canadians. Is this diminished "centre" group among Gen Z indicative of the increasing political polarization we bemoan in society? Or is it simply a function of age—i.e., young people tend to be stereotypically more idealistic, with more strongly held beliefs, before the vicissitudes of life curb their enthusiasm?

Time will tell. But the study clearly identifies a larger pool of self-described right-of-centre voters among Gen Z than among millennials. At the same time, millennials are more likely to go to the polls than Gen Z (71 percent versus 66 percent), and there are more of them that are currently eligible to vote. It is noteworthy that the Liberals' last three electoral victories in 2015, 2019, and 2021 all featured significantly higher participation by voters under the age of thirty-five than the last Conservative majority in 2011 (70–71 percent versus 59 percent). This would suggest that unless the Conservatives can take the millennial vote from the Liberals, or at least get out their accessible millennial voters, high youth participation will work *against* the Tories at the polls.

Voter turnout rates by age group, 2011, 2015, 2019 and 2021 federal elections, %

	2021	2019	2015	2011
Total, all age groups	76	77	77	70
18 to 24 years	66	68	67	55
25 to 34 years	71	71	70	59
35 to 44 years	73	75	75	65
45 to 54 years	76	78	79	73
55 to 64 years	80	81	83	80
65 to 74 years	83	85	86	84
74 years and older	78	79	80	79

Statistics Canada, February 16, 2022, https://www150.statcan.gc.ca/n1/daily-quotidien/220216/cg-d001-eng.htm.

Logically, for the next two federal election cycles, Conservatives should focus on capturing accessible millennial votes if they want to form government. In the decade after that, as Gen Z ages up, Conservatives should revisit that generation to see where their priorities and profiles are and concentrate on securing accessible support.

Based on the nature of the accessible cohorts, this will help accomplish the goal of securing New Canadian support as well as urban support over the longer term. As mentioned earlier, millennials comprise a large part of the urban population. Currently, half the population of downtown Calgary is part of the millennial generation, the highest in the country. In the downtowns of Halifax and Toronto, more than two in five people are millennials.[6] And downtowns are growing fast. According to the 2021 census, from 2016 to 2021, the downtown populations of large urban centres grew faster (by 10.9 percent) than urban centres overall (by 6.1 percent). The populations of downtowns also grew at over twice the pace compared with the previous census cycle (by 4.6 percent).

So how should the Conservative Party approach their accessible millennial and Gen Z voters? In the forward to *GOP GPS: How to Find the Millennials and Urban Voters the Republican Party Needs to Survive*, a book that examines how Republicans might access the youth vote in the United States, American conservative columnist Robert A. George sums up the challenge. "What the millennial, the immigrant, and the general urban dweller have in common is that they're hiding in plain sight. They have their own language(s), culture(s), and dwelling(s) . . . They're open to new takes on old problems—if you (the politician) are willing to see them as they are. Are you willing to withhold judgment? Refrain from imposing your views on them? Well, they may give you a hearing."[7]

Ilona Dougherty agrees. The managing director of the Youth & Innovation Project at the University of Waterloo, Dougherty cofounded Apathy is Boring in 2004 and has advocated for youth engagement ever since. She says the first order of business is listening. "Conservatives need to understand that there is a segment of the youth vote that is accessible to them. What they need to do, number one, is reach out to young voters, ideally in person, but really make young voters a key part of who they connect with. Policy is a little bit secondary—it's about really listening to those voters, because issues are going to change. It's about developing a relationship, it's about listening, it's about really engaging with those young voters so that's the top line."[8]

At the same time, one issue stands out: the economy. "Young voters are struggling economically, so anything that parties can do to address those concerns—be it cost of living, housing, debt—those things are going to resonate with young voters," says Dougherty. "Again, it's about presenting those issues but then having a real conversation with young voters to figure out what message will appeal to them. Things change quickly in this day and age and politicians need to be flexible and agile when responding to their needs."[9]

The first thing youth needs is hope for the future. If every generation wants to do better than their parents, millennials are missing the mark. The recession of 2008–2009 hit just as they were spreading their wings in the workforce, limiting their opportunities. Meanwhile, the cost of housing spiralled. When baby boomers were young adults, it took them an average of five years of full-time work to save for a 20 percent down payment in Toronto, Vancouver, and most major urban centres in Canada. Today, millennials will require fourteen years of full-time work to do the same.[10]

This isn't unique to Canada. In a global study by Deloitte, 29 percent of Gen Z and 36 percent of millennials selected cost of living (defined as housing, transport, bills, etc.) as their greatest concern. "Almost half of Gen Z (46 percent) and millennials (47 percent) live paycheque to paycheque and worry they won't be able to cover their expenses . . . As many as 43 percent of Gen Z and 33 percent of millennials have a second part- or full-time paying job in addition to their primary job. A small but growing percentage are also moving to less expensive cities with remote jobs."[11]

Meanwhile, Gen Z may fare even worse. Even before the current economic downturn and the war in Ukraine, the consensus is that the conditions under which Generation Z is growing up represent "the first time in industrialized history—except for times of war or significant natural disaster—that the financial fortunes of young adults have fallen so far below the rest of society."[12] Part of this is due to the changing nature of work, namely, the "gig economy." Gen Z is more likely than any other age group to be employed in precarious work and multiple jobs, which generally come without benefits or security.

Anger over this situation is starting to be reflected in the polls. According to a study by Nanos Research, both the Conservatives and the NDP have been trending up with younger voters in their weekly surveys. Between February and May 2022, the Tories scored an average of 33 percent with voters aged eighteen to twenty-nine, compared with an average of 25 percent since 2015. Among voters aged thirty to thirty-nine, they garnered 35 percent support over the same period, versus 26 percent for the Liberals.[13] Millennial voters are also souring on the Liberals' potential for fixing the situation. Asked whether they have trust in Trudeau to "create the conditions for economic prosperity," voters eighteen to thirty-four gave him a worse score in 2022 than in 2019—while Gen X and baby boomers gave the Liberals a slightly higher score.[14]

This support may be spilling over to provincial Conservative parties as well. Éric Duhaime, a former radio host and columnist, was elected leader of the Conservative Party of Quebec in 2021. Founded in 2012, the party had not had significant support until this year. Under Duhaime's watch, it has grown to fifty thousand members and sits at second place in the polls behind the governing Coalition Avenir Québec, ahead of the previously dominant Liberal and Parti Québécois parties. Duhaime sees a clear generational divide when it comes to conservatism in his province.

"We're really strong among voters below fifty and we're almost non-existent for those above sixty or sixty-five, which is usually the opposite for conservative parties. We're very strong especially among young families, parents with kids at home, because we talk about freedom and they're the ones who have suffered the most over the last two to three years . . . In contrast, seniors want to give up more of their freedom for government security or accept more intervention of the state in their lives."[15]

Does that mean the Convoy Conservatives are best poised to excite the next generation? The Poilievre campaign would certainly agree. Poilievre himself, while not a millennial, addresses their insecurities about buying a home and making their way in the world. He talks of tech, Bitcoin, and of course, "freedom." So is talk of freedom the key to the youth vote?

Young people are divided on this issue. Remember Tanu Chopra and Jess Goddard from Chapter Eight? Both would fall into the category of "diverse strivers" and both support elements of the Freedom Convoy. "If you want to exercise your own bodily autonomy and not get vaccinated against Covid-19, I do sympathize, especially if you're in a profession like truck driving where you're just going to be alone in a truck all day long," says Goddard. "Why should your job be in jeopardy because of a choice you're making about your body?"[16]

Chopra's view is more nuanced. "I would not categorize my stance as completely aligned with the protesters nor do I support how the protests shaped out in Ottawa. I do, however, believe in their right to protest, and I remain critical of the Liberal government's hypocrisy surrounding the crackdown—both financial and legal—on the protests."[17]

When asked whether her views about the Freedom Convoy translated into support for pro-protest leadership candidates, Chopra said no. "As for who I would support, I remain impressed with Jean Charest's ability and potential to defeat Trudeau. I think he distinguishes himself as a statesman, which in turn casts him in a different light [than] his opponents in the leadership election." But she wasn't sure if the "base" of the party would feel the same way.

Arjun, whom we met in Chapter Seven, was a fan of Poilievre but is now supporting Charest in the current leadership race, in part because he is skeptical of politicians keeping their promises. "If you even asked me a year or two ago, I would have said I could see myself supporting Poilievre . . . I think he did a good job in the shadow cabinet as the shadow finance minister, but over the last year he has been leaning more into populist rhetoric and it seems a little bit disingenuous." Arjun adds, "The reason why I like Jean Charest is because he's always been consistent in what he believes. The policies that he puts forward for this specific leadership race represent a set of values that he's maintained through his entire career. I think that consistency is something that a lot of young voters will value because we distrust a lot of politicians who make promises and don't keep them."

Other young people I spoke with are less concerned about consistency, and more about how a politician addresses the issues of the moment. At a Poilievre rally in downtown Toronto, I met Sako Khederlarian. Sako is thirty-six years old, of Armenian descent, and works at the University of Toronto as an educator and program coordinator in arts-and-dialogue-based programming. Like Chopra, he complained about "woke racism." Khederlarian, however, would be more of a "bro" in terms of his politics. When asked why he was a Conservative, he responded that he was not. He defined himself as progressive and explained that he had voted Liberal, NDP, and Green in previous federal and provincial elections and even spoiled his ballot on one occasion.

So why look at the Tories now? "The mishandling of the trucker protest and the decision to sign an NDP–Liberal coalition were two factors that led me to question the direction of the current government," Khederlarian answered. "I believe the House of Commons needs a strong opposition leader . . . So far, Poilievre has been the most vocal opposition member in the House. I believe if Poilievre represents the interests of Canadians from coast to coast to coast then he can be a successful opposition leader and prime minister."

Like Chopra, Khederlarian was critical of the way the Trudeau government handled the protest. Like Goddard, he thought the government used vaccine mandates as a wedge issue, "instead of speaking with compassion, empathy, and an eye to educate as citizens across the country come to terms with a world that has drastically changed in just two years."[18]

There is clearly a generational difference when it comes to perceptions of Convoy Conservatism. Polls bear this out. Research conducted in May by EKOS[19] found far greater support for the protest movement among Canadians under the age of thirty-five than among older cohorts. Twenty-nine percent of respondents under thirty-five supported the protest versus only 18 percent of those over sixty-five, 21 percent of those aged fifty to sixty-four, and 20 percent of those aged thirty-five to forty-nine. Fifty-eight percent of respondents under thirty-five opposed the convoy, compared to 73 percent of those over sixty-five, and 63–66 percent of those aged thirty-five to sixty-four.[20] Another poll done by Ipsos in early February, a week and a half into the protests, found that 46 percent of Canadians said they "may not agree with everything the people who have taken part in the truck protests in Ottawa have said, but their frustration is legitimate and worthy of our sympathy." A clear majority of eighteen- to thirty-four-year-olds (61 percent) agreed, while those aged thirty-five to fifty-four (44 percent) and fifty-five years old or older (37 percent) were much less likely to agree.[21]

Why were older Canadians less supportive of the convoy than younger Canadians? Criticisms of the Freedom Convoy included the Trumpian and white-supremacist elements in the crowd, the breakdown in law and order in the streets of Ottawa, as well as the economic loss to Canada caused by the border blockades. Could boomers and Gen X have a different personal experience with racism, greater fears about civil unrest, and more at stake in terms of investments or business interests? Could they also have a different perspective on conservatism? Having lived through a time when there was a federal Progressive Conservative Party, Canadians over forty-five have a basis for comparison between populism and conservatism that younger voters lack. Conservatives of that era also know what happens when the Right splits, as it did with Reform, and likely dread another prolonged period of Liberal rule.

These differences could be also because of where young voters get their information. Forget the legacy media preferred by boomers and some of Gen X; for millennials and Gen Z, online news outlets, social media, and YouTube are where it's at.[22] And if you make good use of those spaces, you can reach those younger voters. Even before the current leadership race, one of the candidates had a distinct advantage there, as I learned talking with Gen Z voter Aaron Moore.

Aaron is twenty-four and graduated in 2020 in environmental studies from Brock University, a degree he has since put to use working in water treatment. He grew up in the bedroom community of Courtice outside of Oshawa, Ontario, and currently lives in a small town west of the GTA. When asked to describe himself, he says he cares about Canada and considers himself a "caring person." I'll vouch for that, as

Aaron also happens to be my stepson. We share a love of politics, even when we differ in our opinions, and also, in how we form them.

While Aaron watches *Global*, a traditional news outlet, he mostly consults online sources—and that's where he grew to see and like Pierre Poilievre. "Sometimes I'll just Google the politician and then come up with all the articles. I like YouTube as well—Pierre has his own channel on there . . . Amongst people I know for my age, everyone always talks about Pierre, so I just keep seeing all of the popular media about him. There are tons of videos with tons of views. There's also a very popular Instagram account called 6ixBuzz TV that everyone under thirty in Toronto follows, and they always post stuff about Pierre."[23]

The persona Poilievre has cultivated also resonates with Aaron. "I [saw a video] where he was throwing away pages of a document that were all blacked out, and I remember thinking that no other politician would get up and do that. Everyone's so watchful of what they do, but Pierre does that and has a million views. You don't see these kinds of public figures that are politicians like Pierre."[24]

Young Canadians' definition of conservatism is also more informed by the touchstones of their generation, including American rhetoric and the Harper years, than by the writings of Edmund Burke and the government of Brian Mulroney. Chopra counts *New York Times* columnist Ross Douthat among her influences; both she and Goddard were well aware of Jordan Peterson, but neither had ever heard of Burke. No one had shared with them the conservative concepts of social duty, little platoons, and community responsibility.

Convoy Conservatism and its cry of "freedom" are thus a double-edged sword: they may resonate with many millennials and Gen Z, but have the potential to turn off the Conservatives' more accessible boomer and Gen X voter base. They also fail to capture what younger voters are actually missing—the *opportunity* to climb the economic ladder and make the life they want. The word opportunity, in contrast, encompasses the concerns of both younger and older voters who want that chance for their children. It also addresses the issues of elitism and woke culture, which produce unfair equal outcomes by granting privileged status based on connections, state favour, identity, and/or race.

If Conservatives want to keep the voters they have in the next election and attract the ones they need for the future, it would be wiser to find language that can bridge the concerns of both younger and older voters. In other words, offer the freedom without the fear. And also, show that you take their concerns to heart.

When asked what she wants in a political party, Chopra said, "I want a party that cares." Generally, it is the Left that claims the caring mantle, but Conservatives can—and must—reclaim it. That starts, as Dougherty pointed out, with listening. But it also involves action.

One area where Conservatives can act would be to make life better for young workers in the gig economy. The precarity of work means that young people are unlikely to have workplace benefits such as additional health insurance, retirement plans, or sick days. Government can help by allowing them to keep more of what they earn and save for contingencies or the future, in the form of lower taxes and enhanced savings vehicles (such as an amped-up TFSA).

But they can also go further, like the Ontario Progressive Conservative government of Doug Ford did prior to the 2022 provincial election. After being criticized for inaction during the pandemic, Ford brought in a suite of worker protections including guaranteed sick days. This and other worker-friendly policies helped secure the support of private sector labour unions, a first in a province where unions have traditionally supported the Liberals or the NDP.[25] Ford succeeded in responding to populist demands for change from the working class without tapping into anger and anti-elitism.

Another area Conservatives should act is in improving resources for mental health. Even before the COVID-19 pandemic, young people were experiencing higher levels of anxiety than older Canadians. According to new research by Mental Health Research Canada, the country now faces a new "mental health pandemic," and several groups, including younger Canadians, fare worse than others. Anxiety continues to be more severe for younger Canadians (26 percent of eighteen- to thirty-four-year-olds report anxiety, versus only 12 percent of people over fifty-five) and they are also likely to experience more severe symptoms (51 percent for eighteen- to thirty-four-year-olds, versus 27 percent of those aged fifty-five or older). Younger people are more likely to say their mental health has impacted their ability to function (32 percent of those aged eighteen to thirty-four agree, versus 12 percent of those older than fifty-five).[26] According to the previously cited study by Deloitte, financial stress is one of big drivers for both Gen Z and millennials.[27]

Young people are also hungry for community, which the studies show is an antidote to stress. The Environics / Apathy is Boring study found that only one in six youth "feel a strong sense of belonging to what they define as their local community (typically one's neighbourhood), with more than twice as many describing this connection as somewhat or very weak."[28] Overall life satisfaction was tied to how closely youth feel connected to their local community, even more so than how much income they make. "High life satisfaction is reported by amongst half (48 percent) of those who feel a very strong connection to their local community, dropping to only 18 percent among those with weak connection."[29] That satisfaction was found to be highest among millennial diverse strivers and new traditionalists, as well as Gen Z dutiful accomplishers and hustling hedonists—four groups with a propensity either toward conservative or centrist politics.

This is not surprising. As we know, conservatism is rooted in community and its little platoons. True conservatism finds comfort in tradition and seeks to "conserve" the good in what came before, while adapting to what comes next. Linking the younger generations' desire for community to the worldview of conservatism could make it even more attractive and encourage young people to self-identify as Conservatives.

Unfortunately, politics today is not contributing to that sense of community, at least not in a hands-on way. According to an Elections Canada study of youth-voter turnout, "Fewer than 30 percent of young Canadians under the age of thirty-five reported having been in touch with political parties or candidates during the 2019 campaign, while about 40 percent of Canadians over thirty-five said they had been in touch with a party or a candidate. This finding corroborates prior research and reports showing that young Canadians are much less likely to be contacted and mobilized by political parties before an election . . . which may be one of many factors explaining why youth-turnout rates are much lower than those for older Canadians."[30]

In other words, social media is not enough. Young people need personal connection. And they need it not just with politicians seeking their vote, but with each other.

There is a solution to this, and it starts with the Conservative Party itself: establish a youth wing such as exists in the Liberal and NDP parties and in the former Progressive Conservative Party. This isn't about creating a youth "ghetto," but a community of common interest and experience. It's about finding your crew. And it has long-term implications for the health and longevity of the party. The current leadership race is a perfect example of how loyalties stretch back decades, to the days of the Progressive Conservative Youth Federation. For candidates like Jean Charest and Patrick Brown, it was easy to tap into the networks that they had cultivated since the 1980s and 1990s. As Progressive Conservative leader, Charest interacted directly with the president of the PC Youth Federation, who sat on the party's national council. From 1995 to 1998, that person was me; after that, it was Patrick Brown, who credits Charest as his inspiration for joining the PC party.[31] A youth wing is also a great place to learn valuable campaign skills, find mentorship, and make mistakes with fewer repercussions. Like the municipal farm team, it's a training ground for bigger things.

Finally, climate change and the environment present issues of concern to one of the accessible cohorts for the Conservatives, and to young people generally. No credible national party can hope to form government without a coherent environmental policy. In our next chapter, we will address a holistic approach Conservatives can take to this issue—one that integrates conservation, climate change, energy production, Indigenous reconciliation, and national pride. And if that sounds ambitious, it should be. A political party should offer more than caretaking. It should offer a vision. Young people are looking for hope, growth, and opportunity. Let's give it to them.

— CHAPTER TEN —

THE WEST, THE REST, AND THE BEST:

A NATIONAL VISION FOR NATIONAL UNITY

In a country as diverse as Canada, national visions are sometimes hard to agree on. One region may have completely different values and aspirations from another, due to population, geography, and economic base. Quebec, for example, has cheap and plentiful hydroelectric power, while Alberta is dependent on the petroleum that is the mainstay of its economy. It is easy for Quebecers to be smug about their smaller carbon footprint and oppose pipeline expansion; it is just as understandable that Albertans are proud of their resources and want to get more oil to tidewater. Squaring this circle is no easy task, and one that falls to the federal government. National unity, as we have seen, remains the perennial challenge for every prime minister.

There is one thing most of the country does seem to agree on, however: it resents the concentration of power at its centre, namely, the capital of its largest province, the city of Toronto. This loathing has even been immortalized in film. In a 2007 documentary, *Let's All Hate Toronto*, filmmaker Albert Nerenberg sends a man named Robert Spence across the country on a fake "Toronto Appreciation Day Tour" to find out why

Canadians hate his hometown. From Halifax to Calgary, Spence uncovers the reasons, which include violence, pollution, The Toronto Maple Leafs, and a certain amount of envy for the lifestyles of those living in the Big Smoke. He finds that even Hamilton despises Toronto, resenting that it has a superior football team. In the end, Spence discovers that not only does the rest of the country hate Toronto, but the city has a love–hate relationship with itself.

In political terms, Toronto is a metaphor for something else: the Canadian elite. People who hate the elite do so because they believe that it thinks itself superior and see it as lording this status over the rest of the country. Within the elite itself, there are divisions: not everyone in Toronto, for example, shares in the privilege of its wealthier or more influential citizens. From the outside, it's one big hive of money, hustle, and swagger, but inside, it is a city of contradictions: a magnet for immigrants but a bastion of old money; a vibrant multicultural metropolis but a preserve of old-stock WASPs.

Toronto is also a city of clubs, including the storied Albany Club. Founded in 1882, it was named after Queen Victoria's youngest son, the Duke of Albany; its first honorary president was John A. Macdonald, whose friends and supporters helped form the club. Originally located on Bay Street, the Albany moved to its current location at 91 King Street East in 1898 and has been the nerve centre of Conservative politics ever since.

On a sultry spring evening in May 2022, about two hundred people donned ballgowns and tuxedos for a gala that, for many, was the first such event they had attended since the pandemic shredded their social lives two years prior. In the main dining room, under ceilings resplendent in dark wood panelling, soaring over twenty feet high, and walls painted Farrow and Ball's Stone Blue, guests mingled, toasted old friends, and tucked into their filet mignon. The Club had gathered to honour Jaime Watt, one its former presidents, for his lifetime of service not just to the Albany but to politics and the community at large. Watt is the chairman of Navigator and was one of the architects of the Common Sense Revolution that swept Progressive Conservative premier Mike Harris to power in 1995. He is also one of the greatest philanthropists in the city, if not the country, donating time, money, and professional services to causes including the Shaw Festival, the University Health Network, and Casey House, a specialty AIDS hospital in Toronto. To have Jaime Watt as a friend is a treasure; he is a man of brilliance, integrity, and kindness who has helped thousands of people, from the powerless to the powerful, in time of personal and professional need.

The dinner feting Watt was a who's who of renowned Conservatives including politicians like Harris, former cabinet ministers Lisa MacCormack Raitt, John Baird, and Pauline Browes, organizers such as Walied Soliman, Kory Teneycke, John Capobianco, and Jan Diamond, and fundraisers like Richard Tattersall and John and Nancy McFadyen. There were also a plethora of younger people, some of whom worked at Watt's firm, others who had joined the club in the hope of some-day contributing—and achieving—as much as these older leaders had in their day.

As Watt graciously received his award, one could not help but feel the weight of political gravitas and experience in the room. By any measure, this was the Ontario Conservative elite. The Conservative Party had benefited enormously from their time, talents, and funds over decades. These people had devoted a good part of their lives to the cause of conservative politics. They had won some, they had lost some, but they had persevered and continued to mentor the next generation of Conservatives. Many were involved in the current leadership race. All this was even more remarkable because most of them, like Watt, were also heavily involved in many other interests, on non-profit boards in hospitals and universities, running businesses that created jobs, and devoting time to activities in their local community. They were elites, yes, but they were also good people. The two are not mutually exclusive, as some would have us believe.

Many of the guests didn't start off as elites; they earned their way there through hard work and perseverance. In that room were first- and second-generation Canadians, women, members of the LGBTQ2S+ community, and many others who faced barriers to advancement. I could relate. My parents came here with nothing, sacrificed to put me through private school, and asked only that I work hard, respect my family, and pay it forward—which I chose to do in the form of public service and support for the next generation. They believed that Canada was a land of opportunity, and I still do as well.

If a bomb fell on the Albany that night, a good chunk of the Conservative Party would have been obliterated, and with it, its chances in the next election. A good chunk of people who did a hell of a lot of work in their communities would have been obliterated as well. And yet, bringing down this crowd is precisely what some in the Conservative Party are calling for. Firing the gatekeepers, torching the elites: it's one thing to want to do it to the Liberals, but to your own people? Why? To make some kind of point? To win a leadership? What will you do afterward, when, like in the French Revolution, the heads have rolled, the blood is spilt, and you stand alone in the street with the mob?

The reality is that there are elites in every institution, organization, and society. We have elite athletes. We have elite students. We have elite artists. And yes, we have elite politicians. The goal should not be to eliminate them, but to give everyone a fair shot at becoming them. I don't know a single hockey parent who wouldn't want their kid to go the distance and become an elite player in the NHL. Or a parent who wouldn't be proud if their kid got an award for excellence at school, or won the science fair, or got into a good college. The Canadian Dream is to be able to make a better life for your children. To ensure they have an equal opportunity to excel in whatever field they choose.

National unity depends on that equality of opportunity. The opportunity for francophone Quebecers to achieve their dreams and ambitions. The opportunity for Indigenous people to prosper and thrive. The opportunity for New Canadians to advance without discrimination. The opportunity for Albertans to profit from their resources. And for all, to be able to do it with dignity, and in a way that creates space for the respect of their language, culture, and traditions.

When Canadians say they hate Toronto, when Poilievre supporters say they hate elites, what they're really saying is that they hate unfair unequal outcomes. They hate the thought that unless you're born a rich third-generation Torontonian, you won't have a fair shot at the Canadian Dream. So they turn to populism to remedy the situation. It offers a simple diagnosis—the gatekeepers stand in your way!—and a simple solution. *Remove them!* It is an understandable response when elites lose touch with the Common Sense Canadian, but it doesn't fix the problem, which is a lack, or perceived lack, of social mobility.

If all Canadians had true equality of opportunity, populism wouldn't stand a chance, and we would slay our national unity demons at the same time. That is what the Conservative Party needs to offer all regions of the country. Opportunity is a consistent message that resonates in both official languages, as well as all the other tongues spoken in our land. It resonates across all cultures, and in all regions. It is aspirational. It lifts people up and tells them that they and their children will have the chance to be the elites—to be excellent, and thus have real control over their lives, not by knocking people down but by raising themselves up.

So how do we do this? Let's start in the West. As we saw in Chapter Four, Western Canada has spawned populist movements throughout Canadian history on both the right and the left. From the Socreds to the Progressives to Reform, the West has produced a series of federal parties which have split the centre–right vote. While the NDP, heir to the CCF, has taken the left-leaning vote, this is less consequential, as the centre–left vote has a larger pool to begin with. But for Conservatives, it is deadly; the last split—which produced the Reform Party—led to thirteen years of Liberal rule.

Monte Solberg remembers those days. Solberg was first elected as a Reform Party MP in 1993 and re-elected in 1997; in 2000, he ran and won under the banner of the Canadian Alliance. He subsequently sat briefly as an Independent before joining the Democratic Representative Caucus and was instrumental in the creation of the merged Conservative Party. In 2004, Solberg was elected under its banner and served as minister of citizenship and immigration as well as minister of human resources and social development before retiring in 2008.

Solberg echoes the comments made by Ilona Dougherty with regard to courting young people: the most important thing when it comes to dealing with the West is not to talk but to listen.

"I think part of the answer to dealing with that is to make sure that people feel like they are heard," Solberg ventures. "That doesn't mean that they will necessarily be happy with how governments respond, but it takes away a big argument that they make, which is that the government doesn't listen. Consultation is so important. We talk about it all the time today when dealing with environmental groups, Indigenous groups, all kinds of groups. But when it comes to things like Western alienation, it's sort of like 'you guys are crazy and we don't want to talk to you.'"[1]

This helps explain the visceral reaction to Trudeau's refusal to meet with the protesters at the Freedom Convoy, as well as the support offered up by many Conservative MPs. They saw it as either the right thing to do, or an opportunity to capitalize on Trudeau's refusal to engage, or both. And that is how many Western Conservatives perceived it as well.

Interviewed by *Global News*, Calgary Forest Lawn CPC MP Jasran Singh Hallan suggested the government "extend an olive branch" to the protesters. "Let's get together and listen . . . Let's figure out what is it that they really want, because no one wants to continue with these demonstrations. Everyone wants these demonstrations to end."[2] CPC interim leader Candice Bergen wrote to Prime Minister Justin Trudeau calling for a meeting of party leaders to discuss ways to "de-escalate the protests." Calgary MP Stephanie Kusie tweeted support for the idea, saying, "I'm tired of this situation being used for political gain on any side. We have a number of significant problems facing us as a nation that we need to address without the political games distracting us. Let's come together and discuss a plan for the betterment of Canada."[3]

The government, of course, did not accede to these requests. Trudeau had drawn a line in the sand on the convoy, condemning it and calling for it to end. As polls bore out, his condemnation was shared by a large majority of Liberal voters as well as a smaller majority of the population at large. Because of the convoy's Western origins, however, his intransigence was also seen as a slap against the West, adding further fuel to the prairie brushfire that is Western alienation.

Western alienation, and its more extreme cousin, Western separatism, have waxed and waned over the decades, and while Justin Trudeau fanned its flames, he cannot take all the blame (or credit) for it. Trudeau wasn't the one who ousted Alberta premier Jason Kenney in the hopes of replacing him with a more radical voice, for example; Albertan Conservatives did that to themselves. Two people who arguably contributed the most to Western alienation were Pierre Elliott Trudeau with his National Energy Program, which spawned the famous bumper sticker "Let the Eastern Bastards Freeze in the Dark," and John Diefenbaker, who conceived Canada's first equalization program in 1957, including an "Atlantic provinces adjustment grant."[4] Both initiatives were populist— attempting to provide cheap energy to the masses, as well as money to regions of the country that were suffering economically. And both were incredibly divisive.

Healing those divisions starts with something that is a conservative principle: devolution of powers and decentralization. Conservative government, as we have seen, is local government. Devolving different powers to different provinces based on their individual needs is not an abdication of federal responsibility but a recognition of the diversity of the country. Solberg sees it this way:

"Maybe it's less about institutional change and more of a recognition of the division of powers in the Constitution, sections 91 and 92, and ensuring that Alberta has control over its natural resources. Part of the answer is to ensure that there's more autonomy under the current division of powers, and there does seem to be some favouritism toward Quebec."[5]

Solberg is not wrong: Quebec has always been at the centre of the question of division of powers when it comes to federal politics. At the same time, there are limits to how much can be given over. Pandering is not the answer. In the words of Senator Leo Housakos, you can't "out-nationalist the nationalists" when it comes to Quebec.[6] In the last election, the Conservative Party promised a "contract with Quebec" that they promised to enact within one hundred days. It did little to increase the party's popularity in the province. Why? Because of the phenomenon known as "parking your vote." And the biggest parking lot Quebecers have right now is the Bloc Québécois.

According to Conservative Party of Quebec leader Éric Duhaime, "The Bloc has always been a parking lot for people who didn't know where to go. People are still parked there and looking at the other options, so the Bloc survived. People are waiting something for something to happen . . . Is there ever going to be a clear conservative alternative that's going to be able to excite people? I think so."

What could excite them? According to Duhaime, the party needs an appeal rooted in conservative principles, both cultural and fiscal. "People feel that they are being pushed and their politicians are trying to change their lifestyle and traditions. I think Pierre [Poilievre] was able to touch that. He represents a kind of a breath of fresh air, he speaks like he thinks, without the 'woke' and the political correctness," Duhaime continued. "There's also economic insecurity, people are really afraid because all those changes are also affecting their wallets . . . A young family could not afford to buy a house if they don't have one already or if their parents are not wealthy, the gas price and everything is going up, there's a huge insecurity of what the future is going to look like."

What Duhaime cautions against, however, is a focus on social conservatism. "There's not a lot of room for social conservatism in Quebec. That's something very different [about our party]: the fact that I'm openly gay, the fact that you know we're pro-choice or pro–gay rights. All the issues that have been very divisive on this at the federal level are not really an issue in Quebec."

In other words, emphasize what you can agree on, not that on which you disagree. As long as the party continues to represent a "parking lot" for Quebec voters who don't like the Liberals, but can't bring themselves to vote Conservative, it will stymie Tory efforts to regain power. Conservatives need to win Quebec if they want to form a majority government. On rare occasions such as the 2011 election, they have won without significant support in "La Belle Province," but that election also saw the NDP sweep the province and Liberals fall to their lowest seat count in history, a scenario that is unlikely to repeat itself.

Winning Quebec also requires understanding Quebec—not just speaking the language. Quebec society is distinct in myriad ways, from its institutions such as the Caisse de dépôt et placement du Québec (CDPQ) to its star system and entertainment culture. It is no accident that party leaders who hail from the province have an advantage over those who don't. Unless you've grown up or spent a significant part of your life in the province, it is very difficult to appreciate its worldview.

Prime Minister Brian Mulroney was the last Tory leader to carry the province, as a Progressive Conservative; since then, it has provided the necessary support for the Liberal governments of Jean Chrétien and Justin Trudeau, both seen as native sons.

Given Canada's regional disparities, does the route to power run through the middle? Is centre-right the space to occupy, not the right alone? In conversation with former Conservative cabinet ministers Peter MacKay and John Baird, both agreed that a measure of compromise will be necessary to win. "Somewhere in all these considerations is, do we want to be in government?" asks MacKay. "We can rail at the moon and play footsie with social issues and bring back those discussions, but it will alienate voters and make us unelectable. We've had three elections now that demonstrate the truth of what I'm saying. We cannot be out on the fringes and govern in a country like ours. Somewhere there have to be compromises."[7]

Baird puts it this way: "There's nothing wrong with compromising as long as compromising doesn't become an ideology in itself." At the same time, he emphasizes, "We win elections when we run as conservatives. We've got to make the conservative case, we've got to lead, and tell Canadians why the reckless and irresponsible spending of the last two years is bad, how it hurts Canadian families, show the scale of the debt, how it leads to a lower quality of life."[8]

Navigating the divide between social and fiscal conservatives is one thing; navigating the new class divide between Convoy and Club Conservatives is another. The convoy exposed fault lines that most observers agree will be difficult to heal. And the party has to mend from the ground up rather than simply look to its leader for salvation. In Baird's view, "Too much thought is always gone into who shall be leader, rather than what kind of party shall they lead."[9]

MacKay offered these thoughts: "I'm not advocating for the Progressive Conservative positioning of a Joe Clark, but a more centrist position that supports law and order, is for lower taxes [and] fiscal responsibility, and recognize[s] the difference in the country between urban and rural. I see myself as a conservative from the Mulroney and Don Mazankowski era. We need to get those switchers."[10]

There is another way to overcome old internal divisions: give people something *new* behind which they can unite. Pierre Elliott Trudeau did this in the 1970s with his federal multiculturalism policy. Apart from attracting newcomers to the Liberal Party, it was designed to change the conversation and take the spotlight off the Quebec sovereignty movement—to give people something else to talk about. It succeeded on both counts, and the Liberals have benefited from its repercussions to this day.

In 2022, the Conservatives need to find their own national vision to change the conversation. The good news is that there is one already on the table that is not only perfect for the party but for the country as well. It would reconcile resource development and climate change action; it would create jobs and prosperity; it would bridge East and West; and it would engage Indigenous voters. It would also instill pride and hope and raise Canada's stature in the world.

That vision is of Canada as a global energy superpower. This vision is already on the lips of several candidates in the current leadership race: Jean Charest has a fulsome plan on the subject; Pierre Poilievre talks of supplying energy to Europe; and Roman Baber talks of critical minerals and electrification. If there is a vision that could unite the party and heal both its divisions and those of the country, a pan-Canadian energy vision would be it.

What would such a vision look like? For starters, it would encompass both traditional fossil fuels and renewables like electrification and hydrogen. Canada and the world need both. It is illogical to abandon the first when the second is still under development; no matter how much environmentalists would like to speed things up, the reality is that Canada will not achieve net zero for decades to come.

Mac Van Wielingen concurs. Dubbed "Calgary's corporate radical,"[11] Van Wielingen is the founder and chair of Viewpoint Group, co-founder of asset-management firm Viewpoint Investment Partners (VIP), and a partner in ARC Financial Corporation, the largest private-equity investment management company in Canada focused on the energy sector. He is also founder and current chair of the Business Council of Alberta. In 2021, he authored a University of Calgary report on the future pathway for Canada's energy sector.[12]

"We're now starting to get more grounded," Van Wielingen says. "Whereas over the last number of years we had quite an inexplicable number of people, including even in Ottawa, who seemed to think that this could be done in relatively short order—within ten years—it will be multidecadal and people really don't like it when I also say probably even multigenerational."[13]

How does the energy sector feel about this? Van Wielingen is optimistic. "I can say with certainty that the oil and gas sector in Canada is committed to reduce emissions. They are totally focused on reducing emissions, they are not resisting it." The other side, however, may be a different story. "With respect to the activist community, that is a real conundrum. They've gotten so mobilized and so focused and I say this to them, there's a rigidity of perspective that is going to undermine their own credibility and I think it will continue to unless they can open up and be a little bit more flexible, as they consider time frames and substitutes."[14]

A Conservative policy would start with the repeal of Bills C-69 and C-48, legislation that stymies the development of infrastructure necessary to carry petroleum products to markets, as well as the export of these commodities, including liquefied natural gas (LNG) to Europe. At the same time, the oil and gas industry must commit to reducing emissions through the acceleration of carbon-capture technology and carbon dioxide–removal technology. This would be incentivized by the repeal of the current Liberal carbon tax and replacement with an industrial carbon price, one of the ideas put forward by Charest and developed in consultation with the Conservatives for their Clean Growth initiative.[15] Finally, Canada needs to ramp up production of critical minerals needed for electrification, and of the cleanest possible hydrogen, a means of offsetting emissions from fossil fuels and thereby reducing our overall carbon dioxide footprint.

When it comes to critical minerals necessary for electric vehicle production, most industry watchers agree that the moment to act is now. The consulting firm McKinsey & Company projects that the global market for battery cells will grow about twenty percent every year to US$360 billion in 2030, while the World Bank estimates global demand for critical minerals could expand by 500 percent within the next thirty years.[16]

Canada has reserves of critical minerals including lithium, nickel, and cobalt in many places, one such site being the Ring of Fire in Northern Ontario. But mining is a notoriously risky business, and without incentives for the private sector, development will not occur. In an interview with the *Toronto Star* in 2022, Pierre Gratton, president and chief executive officer of the Mining Association of Canada, said the government should put more money into geological surveying and increase exploration tax credits; during the 2021 election, the Liberals promised to double a tax credit for critical mineral exploration. Gratton described this as "a huge thing. That would help find those new mines we need to find if we're going to produce the quantities we need for electric vehicle batteries."

Increased LNG production and critical-minerals extraction are not only priorities for energy production but for national and international security. The war in Ukraine has exposed the need for Europe to diversify its energy sources beyond Russia, while Canada and the world require stable sources of critical minerals other than China, which currently has 35 percent of mineral reserves worldwide and accounts for 70 percent of global production.[17] Canada needs to rigorously review foreign investment in the sector to ensure our national interest is protected.

Several leadership candidates have talked about creating a national infrastructure corridor to connect key resource regions with critical infrastructure using a single expedited regulatory process. Charest's vision encompasses infrastructure connections including a hydro corridor from Labrador through to Ontario and the Maritimes, the Ring of Fire, the Arctic Gateway to Churchill, Manitoba, and getting Alberta oil and gas to tidewater. Poilievre speaks of reviving projects such as Energy East to get LNG to European markets.

None of this will get done, however, without the buy-in of Canada's Indigenous Peoples. True reconciliation is about more than just apologies—it's about wealth creation. The term "economic reconciliation" encompasses inclusion, development, and control over resources.

The mining sector is currently the largest employer of Indigenous people, with over five hundred deals signed between First Nations and resource companies. There is space for much more.

Gerry St. Germain agrees. The former senator is a member of the Métis Nation and the founder of the First Nations Major Projects Coalition. For decades, he has campaigned tirelessly for the rights and recognition of Indigenous Peoples. He also believes in the importance of equality of opportunity when it comes to realizing those aspirations.

"Until Indigenous people are given a proper opportunity within the mainstream of our modern economy, they will not truly be able to take their rightful place in Canadian society. They must become active participants in the business affairs of our country."[18]

What does that look like in practice? "That means inviting First Nations to participate with equity investments, with secure and ongoing financing provided by the federal and provincial governments, in corporations, joint ventures, and other business transactions. They must be represented on corporate boards and recruited to C-suite positions in major corporations. From their investment and corporate activities, reliable streams of revenue will flow and will grow to allow them to strategically plan for their futures."[19]

St. Germain believes that a holistic approach is key to moving forward while respecting traditional Indigenous ways of life. It would also benefit all of Canada in terms of environmental protection.

"From the time of first contact, Indigenous people watched as their economy was destroyed by the new arrivals. That economy thrived and supported their way of life for thousands of years, based on the careful stewardship of local renewable resources, in harmony with the forces of nature. I am confident the active involvement of Indigenous people in the mainstream economy will help demonstrate to Canadians how we all can live in harmony with Mother Nature, and understand that we must not try to conquer nature because we are *all* of nature."[20]

Several leadership candidates have underlined the importance of Indigenous engagement and economic reconciliation. Poilievre has met with chiefs in Northern and Southern Alberta to discuss how encouraging resource development could benefit their people. Charest proposes working with First Nations across Canada to create and fund a federal Indigenous opportunities corporation, based on the Alberta model, to provide loan guarantees and other support to Indigenous groups, allowing them to invest in Canadian resource projects and build prosperity for their people.

Developing Canada's resources sector is a cross-jurisdictional initiative. It requires the engagement of the private sector, workers, communities, and multiple levels of government. It also draws on a rich historical tradition of which Canada should be proud, not defensive. Resources have been the backbone of our economy since before Confederation. Now, Canada is in a unique position to help the world reduce its carbon footprint, a fact we should celebrate and champion at home and abroad.

Van Wielingen is optimistic, and shares St. Germain's vision of a synergy between the economy, the energy sector, and the environment. "I do believe this is the future of conservative thought—to think holistically. We got truncated into focusing on economic priorities, and business leaders would say we create wealth and we create jobs—it was insufficient for people . . . The real mistake Conservatives made going back to 2019 was downplaying the environment. It was alienating for young people. We need national political leaders to stand up and face the world and extol the positive attributes of Canada's energy-and-resources sector—we are among the most responsible energy-and-resource developers—but with full knowledge of emissions challenges. We need to be deeper on some of the other aspirational areas that are so important."[21]

Taking forward a vision of this scale will require leadership. It will require experience. It will require capital and social licence. In other words, it will require both the elite and the grassroots to cooperate rather than fight each other. And it will require politicians to bring people together instead of pitting them against each other, especially within the same party.

What could inspire support for this vision and bridge the two solitudes of populism and conservatism? Apart from opportunity, there is another value to consider: patriotism. When I asked two young people from completely different backgrounds and opposing leadership camps why they defined themselves as Conservatives, they both gave the same answer: pride in their country.

Aaron, our Gen Z Poilievre fan, who can trace his family back six generations in rural Ontario, said, "I think, to me, Conservatives probably care more about their country . . . They're people who want to preserve the ways of their country, unlike the Liberals and the NDP. I associate with that growing up here, being born here, especially being a guy. I feel like the Conservative Party is speaking to me."

Arjun, the Indian immigrant and Charest supporter who grew up in the GTA, said, "I am a Conservative for two reasons: personal responsibility, and patriotism, the ability to be proud of your country. I think that's one of the things that historically founded the Conservative Party. I like that we are all able to share in the national Canadian story and be part of the Canadian identity."

Canada and the Conservative Party are intimately connected. Our party was instrumental in its founding; our first prime minister was a Conservative. Maintaining the unity of a nation with so many challenges both from without and within has been both a trial and a triumph. On the world stage, Canada is emblematic of what can be achieved when people put aside their differences to live peaceably with one another. We are not perfect, but we never stop trying. Conservatives must remain at the forefront of this endeavour and wave the flag proudly, not as a symbol of Convoys, or Clubs, but of Canada, the true shining city on the hill, a place of peace, order, good government, and hope for the world.

Dear Conservatives, let's preach love, not hate. Let's stand up for our country instead of tearing each other down. Let's stop demonizing the elites, because—like in Nerenberg's documentary—we end up hating only ourselves. Instead, let's work together. Let's talk about opportunity. Let's talk about patriotism. Let's talk about national vision. Let's chart the right path. Let's create a Conservative Party that provides a real alternative to the Liberal status quo, that can win the next election, that offers a brighter future for our country and our children, and that unites, inspires, and takes Canada forward.

RETURN OF THE LIBERAL–CONSERVATIVE PARTY?

"The impossibility of conservatism in our era is the impossibility of Canada. As Canadians we attempted a ridiculous task in trying to build a conservative nation in the age of progress, on a continent we share with the most dynamic nation on earth. The current of modern history was against us."[1]

Most observers agree that there are two likely outcomes to the current leadership race: either the Conservative Party elects a leader that positions it as a big-tent centre–right vehicle, or one who takes a more populist path. Whichever result prevails, based on the current bitter climate in this contest, it will be very difficult for supporters of one faction to live in harmony with the other. Candidates are calling each other liars. Patrick Brown has declared he will not run under Pierre Poilievre. A centrist party will alienate populists. A populist party will alienate centrists. And so on.

There is a third possibility. Canadian politics may come full circle, back to the party that founded the country: the Liberal–Conservative Party.

Across the country, parties are rising and falling. In Quebec, the once mighty Liberal and PQ parties are shadows of their former selves.

Vying for the crown in the next provincial election are three new vehicles: the Coalition Avenir Québec, Québec Solidaire, and the Conservative Party. In Alberta, the Conservative vote has split and reformed into the Conservative Party, the Maverick Party, and the United Conservative Party.

A Liberal–Conservative party would not be a coalition of the two existing political organizations. Macdonald's original party represented a synergy of classical liberalism with conservative thought, in the mould of the former federal Progressive Conservative Party. It would be neither statist nor populist. It would straddle the centre=right and appeal to the Common Sense Canadian voter. It would provide a home for disaffected Blue Liberals and Red Tories. It would counter populism not by rejecting "elites" but by creating a culture of opportunity. It would unite the country geographically and demographically, by appealing to East and West, New and Old Canadians.

Such a party could be achieved in one of two ways: the Conservative Party elects a centre–right leader who builds the party in this image. Or, if such a leader does not prevail, a new party is created, with a new name and a new brand, to be determined.

Brands can be both an advantage and an albatross. As the Poilievre campaign has shown, redefining your brand can attract people who don't subscribe to labels. Meanwhile, there is comfort in the familiar. People who have been involved in politics for a long time feel like they are part of a family. While you may attract new people, you want to retain the old too.

A new party also brings the very real threat of another prolonged Liberal reign. As we have seen, every time the Conservative amoeba splits, the Liberal Party fills the space. That is not in Canadians' interest. In order to have a healthy democracy, they need a choice of governing parties.

The goal of politics is not to cling to ideology, but to use it to make life better for people. Governing is a constant tension between the poles of freedom and security. Veer too far either way, and trouble takes hold. Anarchy and dictatorship are not polar opposites but kissing cousins—both the product of a failure of leadership and a failure to find political consensus.

Benjamin Disraeli, Conservative prime minister of Great Britain, said many smart things, including two that apply to our current situation:

"In a progressive country, change is constant . . . change is inevitable."[2]

And,

"I am a Conservative to preserve all that is good in our constitution, a radical to remove all that is bad."[3]

This is not about creating a mushy middle. This is about building a party that can find consensus on the big challenges of the day and forge a path. The right path, one that addresses the key issues Canada has faced since its creation: the challenge of national unity. Whether unity of French and English, New and Old Canadian, First Peoples and Founding Peoples, East and West, the challenge for politicians remains the same: how to bring and keep people together so the country does not fall apart.

This does not mean that every single element should be brought into the tent. Elements that divide, whether woke or populist, won't find a home there. Radical or fringe groups, ditto. This is about finding common ground with Common Sense Canadians, or enough of them, at least, to get things done.

And there are many things that need doing. Canada needs to improve productivity. We need to tackle inflation. We need to square the circle of energy and the environment. We need to reconcile with Indigenous Peoples. We need to address the issues of automation, the gig economy, generational inequities, and political polarization.

Canada doesn't need more freedom. Canada needs more opportunity. The pandemic will end, and with it, the mandates that have constrained and frustrated all of us to varying degrees. But opportunity isn't a given, and it demands attention.

In a modern state, opportunity comes from both the private and public sectors; they are interdependent. The private sector cannot flourish if the public sector crowds it out. But it also relies on the public sector to operate efficiently and maintain services it cannot provide. National security and law and order top this list. Without a functioning legal system, the private sector cannot enforce contracts. Without strong defence, our nation will not be secure. Rules, and the upholding of rules, must be clear. Investors must be confident that they can come to Canada and prosper. Rules must be fair, predictable, and not overly restrictive. Environmental restrictions should not be so limiting that they drive away investment. Innovation should not be stifled by red tape.

This does not mean discarding the "gatekeepers." There will always be gates. A society does not function without them. Gates are not about elites. Gates are about ensuring that standards are upheld. Gates include contract laws that ensure suppliers are paid, building codes so apartments don't collapse, health inspections so restaurants don't have rats in the kitchen. Gates should not be too restrictive, or too numerous, but they are necessary for a functioning society. To say otherwise is pure demagoguery.

Government's role does not lie in removing gatekeepers. It lies in building fair gates and providing more keys. That's where the public sector, through the delivery of health, education, and infrastructure, plays a role. There will be no Ring of Fire without roads. There will be no engineers or plumbers without training. There will be no workforce without health.

Keys unlock opportunity. They are the true means of raising up the working class. They create social mobility. They are the true antidote to populism.

A vibrant centre–right Conservative Party could provide those keys. A vibrant centre-right Liberal-Conservative party could provide them as well, but might face an uphill battle for power. Ultimately, though, labels shouldn't matter. Leadership should. True leaders show the way to a better future, to unity and growth. And that will be the right path, for Conservatives and for Canada.

ACKNOWLEDGMENTS

Thanks to my literary agent, Sam Hiyate, for nearly twenty years of friendship and representation, and who believed in this book from the start. To my publisher and friend, Dean Baxendale, who did the same; thank you for all your encouragement and for leading such a great team at Optimum. To wonderful and patient editors Margo LaPierre and Janice Weaver, thank you for your sharp minds, sharp pens, and quick turnaround. Great thanks to the fabulous Lisa MacCormack Raitt for writing the foreword; knowing all the other commitments you have, it means so much.

Thanks to Chairman Jaime Watt and the team at Navigator, for giving me the space to complete this project and for being the most understanding and supportive boss and colleague one could ever hope to have. Thanks to Thomas Ashcroft, who contributed ideas, writing, and research on urban issues, and Zeus Eden, for research on critical minerals. Special thanks to Philippe Gervais and Randy Dawson, for leading my exploratory team in the leadership frenzy; you went above and beyond the call of friendship and I am ever in your debt.

Thanks to all the people I spoke with whose voices find themselves on these pages, as well as those whose input wasn't quoted here: you all helped shape this narrative and it was an honour to engage with you. Additional research shout-outs go to Ilona Dougherty, for providing priceless insights into the minds of young voters, and to Fraser Macdonald, on how to make Canada a global energy superpower. Thank you as well to all the endorsers and supporters of the book, on the jacket, on air, and online.

As a single parent, I have to give the greatest thanks to the village: my mother, Rita Kheiriddin, whose support and love have blessed me for the past fifty-two years; my dear daughter, Zara, who put up with Mummy's absence both mental and physical (me: "I'm so sorry, sweetheart, I feel like I missed four months of your life," Zara: "Yeah, Mom, you did, but it's okay"); my former partner, Bill Moore, for being a great stepdad to Z, be it at skating practice, carpool, or just in general. Thanks to my friends: Elisabeth Schorsch for juggling the school run and giving great parenting advice; to Katarina and Drago Banovic and their girls for giving Zara fun time while I was writing; to Carrie Hughes-Grant for that lifesaving sleepover; to Véronique Malka, Anie Perrault, Marcella Munro, Sujata Raisinghani and Jane Fairburn for moral support and always having my back; to Marla McAlpine, Graydon Moffat, Elen Steinberg, Jill Harvey, Aphrodite Salas, and Caroline Miller for their kindness, encouragement, late-night chats, and supportive texts throughout this process.

Finally, to all the members of the Conservative Party of Canada, thank you for your dedication to the cause of conservatism in particular and politics in general. Without your engagement, there would be no party to write about. I hope this book helps us take it forward and give Canada the best government it can have, for ourselves and for our children.

ABOUT THE AUTHOR

TASHA KHEIRIDDIN is an accomplished journalist and author with over twenty years of media, policy, and communications experience. She co-wrote *Rescuing Canada's Right: Blueprint for a Conservative Revolution*, with journalist Adam Daifallah. Over the course of her media career, she hosted *The Tasha Kheiriddin Show* on Global News Radio, co-hosted CTV News Channel's *National Affairs*, and served as a member of the editorial board and columnist at the *National Post*, a columnist at iPolitics.ca, a producer with CBC Newsworld, and an award-winning host-producer at the Cable Public Affairs Channel. In 2016, the Women's Executive Network named Tasha one of Canada's "Top 100 Most Powerful Women" for her work in media and communications.

NOTES

Introduction: The Day Trump Came to Canada

1. Tom Yun, "Donald Trump Voices Support for Truckers Convoy Protest in Ottawa," *CTV News*, January 29, 2022, https://www.ctvnews.ca/canada/donald-trump-voices-support-for-truckers-convoy-protest-in-ottawa-1.5760331.

2. "History Through Our Eyes: June 25, 1968: Trudeau Doesn't Flinch," *Montreal Gazette*, June 25, 2019, https://montrealgazette.com/news/local-news/history-through-our-eyes/history-through-our-eyes-june-25-1968-trudeau-doesnt-flinch.

3. Christopher Nardi, "Not 'Intimidated' by Protesters: Trudeau Says He Will Not Meet with Trucker Convoy Organizers," *National Post*, January 31, 2022, https://nationalpost.com/news/politics/not-intimidated-by-protesters-trudeau-says-he-will-not-meet-with-trucker-convoy-organizers.

4. Anne Caroline Desplanques, "'Convoi de la Liberté': Quand la Liberté Est Plutôt un Gros Free-for-All," *Le Journal de Montréal*, January 30, 2022, https://www.journaldemontreal.com/2022/01/30/quand-la-liberte-est-plutot-un-gros-free-for-all.

5. Brooklyn Neustaeter and Matthew Talbot, "Timeline: Trucker Convoy Protest in Ottawa," *CTV News*, January 29, 2022, https://www.ctvnews.ca/politics/timeline-trucker-convoy-protest-in-ottawa-1.5759806.

6. Nicole Thompson, "Officials Decry 'Desecration' of Monuments During Ottawa Protest," *National Newswatch*, January 29, 2022, https://www.nationalnewswatch.com/2022/01/29/officials-decry-desecration-of-monuments-during-ottawa-protest/#.YfaI9-rMK5e.

7. Pierre Poilievre (@PierrePoilievre), "BREAKING: Another Liberal turns on Trudeau's nasty and divisive pandemic politics. The people's voices are triumphing. Sign my petition to add your voice to restoring freedom: [Quoted, Pierre Poilievre for Prime Minister: End Mandates, Passports and Restrictions]," Twitter, February 9, 2022, 3:00 p.m., https://twitter.

com/pierrepoilievre/status/1491502258948816905?lang=zh-Hant.

8. Parliamentary Precinct, "Pierre Poilievre on the Canadian Freedom Convoy 2022," Question Period for HoC Sitting No. 20 House of Commons, January 31, 2022, YouTube video, 6:31, https://www.youtube.com/watch?v=WFdT75gDwiQ.

9. Idil Mussa, "Do You Have a Permit for That? NCC Shuts Down Kids' Lemonade Stand," *CBC News*, July 3, 2016, https://www.cbc.ca/news/canada/ottawa/ottawa-ncc-shuts-down-lemonade-stand-1.3662830.

10. Aedan Helmer, "Convoy Organizer Pat King Facing New Perjury, Obstruction Charges, Bail Review Hearing Delayed," *Ottawa Citizen*, April 14, 2022, https://ottawacitizen.com/news/local-news/pat-king-returns-to-court-for-bail-review-after-abrupt-adjournment.

11. Alex Boutilier, "Domestic Extremism 'Here to Stay' in Canada, Trudeau's Security Advisor Says," *Global News*, March 10, 2022, https://globalnews.ca/news/8673217/domestic-extremism-here-to-stay-in-canada-trudeaus-security-advisor-says/.

12. Nick Tailor-Vaisey, "Running on Empty," *Politico*, January 31, 2022, https://www.politico.com/newsletters/ottawa-playbook/2022/01/31/running-on-empty-00003535.

13. Jennifer La Grassa, "Ambassador Bridge Blockade Stalled Billions in Trade—and There Could Be Other Effects: Expert," *CBC News*, February 15, 2022, https://www.cbc.ca/news/canada/windsor/ambassador-bridge-protest-cost-1.6351312.

14. "Ambassador Bridge Blockade Response Cost City of Windsor $5.7M," *CBC News*, March 15, 2022, https://www.cbc.ca/news/canada/windsor/windsor-blockade-cost-1.6385826.

15. Adam Toy, "Four Charged with Conspiracy to Murder after Raid on Coutts Blockade," *Global News*, February 15, 2022, https://globalnews.ca/news/8622765/conspiracy-to-murder-weapons-chargers-coutts-blockade-raid/.

16. David Friend and Amy Smart, "Harassment, Threats to Journalists During Protests Are Dangerous, Say Experts," *Global News*, February 21, 2022, https://globalnews.ca/news/8635223/harassment-threats-journalists-freedom-convoy-protests/.

17. Stephanie Levitz, "'Yes to Peaceful Protests': Pierre Poilievre Doubles Down on Support for Ottawa Demonstrators," *Toronto Star*, February 14, 2022, https://www.thestar.com/politics/federal/2022/02/14/yes-to-peaceful-protests-pierre-poilievre-doubles-down-on-support-for-ottawa-demonstrators.html.

18. Darrell Bricker, "Nearly Half (46%) of Canadians Say They 'May not

Agree with Everything' Trucker Convoy Says or Does, But . . ." *Ipsos*, February 11, 2022, https://www.ipsos.com/en-ca/news-polls/nearly-half-say-they-may-not-agree-with-trucker-convoy.

19. Stephanie Levitz, "Pierre Poilievre's Campaign Claims Record-Breaking Conservative Memberships Sales in Bid for Party Leadership," *Toronto Star*, June 4, 2022, https://www.thestar.com/politics/federal/2022/06/04/pierre-poilievres-campaign-claims-record-breaking-conservative-memberships-sales-in-bid-for-party-leadership.html.

20. Gary Mason, "How Truck Convoy Supporters Like Pierre Poilievre Have Weaponized 'Freedom,'" *The Globe and Mail*, February 8, 2022, https://www.theglobeandmail.com/opinion/article-the-alt-right-has-weaponized-freedom-to-undermine-democracy/.

21. Melanie Zanona, "Republican Leaders Face Threat of Revived Freedom Caucus in GOP-Led House," *CNN*, March 8, 2022, https://www.cnn.com/2022/03/08/politics/house-freedom-caucus-revived-republican-majority/index.html.

22. Lee Moran, "Rep. Lauren Boebert Ridiculed for Hot Take on Ukraine and Guns," *HuffPost*, March 8, 2022, https://news.yahoo.com/rep-lauren-boebert-ridiculed-hot-083504616.html.

23. Roxanne Roberts, "Hillary Clinton's 'Deplorables' Speech Shocked Voters Five Years Ago—But Some Feel It Was Prescient," *The Washington Post*, August 31, 2021, https://www.washingtonpost.com/lifestyle/2021/08/31/deplorables-basket-hillary-clinton/.

24. Jamie Watt, "The Pandemic Has Emboldened Supporters of the People's Party of Canada. Whoever Forms Government Will Need to Contend with Them for Years to Come," *Toronto Star*, September 19, 2021, https://www.thestar.com/opinion/contributors/2021/09/19/the-pandemic-has-emboldened-supporters-of-the-peoples-party-of-canada-whoever-forms-government-will-need-to-contend-with-them-for-years-to-come.html.

25. "Canadians Support Democrat John Kerry for Next US President," *Ipsos Reid*, July 27, 2004, https://www.ipsos.com/en-ca/canadians-support-democrat-john-kerry-next-us-president.

26. "Nine in Ten (90%) Canadians Believe Barack Obama Will Retain Presidency and 86% Would Vote for Obama If They Could," *Ipsos*, November 3, 2012, https://www.ipsos.com/en-ca/nine-ten-90-canadians-believe-barack-obama-will-retain-presidency-and-86-would-vote-obama-if-they.

27. "Leger's Weekly Survey," *The Canadian Press*, November 2, 2020, https://2g2ckk18vixp3neolz4b6605-wpengine.netdna-ssl.com/wp-content/uploads/2020/11/Legers-Weekly-Survey-November-2nd-2020-min-1.pdf.

28. John Ibbitson, "The Politics of 2036, When Canada Is as Brown as It Is White," *The Globe and Mail,* January 27, 2017, https://www.theglobeandmail.com/news/politics/the-politics-of-2036-when-canada-is-as-brown-as-it-is-white/article33814437/.

29. "Canada's Cities Are About to Add Millions of New Residents. They Can't All Drive to Work," *The Globe and Mail,* January 3, 2020, https://www.theglobeandmail.com/opinion/editorials/article-canadas-cities-are-about-to-add-millions-of-new-residents-they-cant/.

Chapter One: The Harper Years: Recasting the Canadian Narrative

1. Bob Plamondon, *Blue Thunder: The Truth About Conservatives from Macdonald to Harper* (Toronto: Key Porter Books, 2009), 25–26.

2. Plamondon, *Blue Thunder,* 26.

3. Plamondon, 27.

4. Paul Wells, *Right Side Up: The Fall of Paul Martin and the Rise of Stephen Harper's New Conservatism* (Toronto: Douglas Gibson Books, 2007), 11.

5. Wells, *Right Side Up,* 12.

6. Bob Plamondon, *Full Circle: Death and Resurrection in Canadian Conservative Politics* (Toronto: Key Porter Books, 2009), 115.

7. Preston Manning, *The New Canada* (Toronto: Macmillan of Canada, 1991), 26.

8. Plamondon, *Full Circle,* 98.

9. John Ibbitson, *Stephen Harper* (Toronto: Signal Books, 2015), 230.

10. Ibbitson, *Stephen Harper,* 117.

11. Plamondon, 222.

12. Ibbitson, 185.

13. Ibbitson, 227.

14. Plamondon, *Blue Thunder,* 440.

15. Ibbitson, 249.

16. Paul Wells, *The Longer I'm Prime Minister: Stephen Harper and Canada, 2006–* (Toronto: Random House Canada, 2013), 80.

17. Jennifer Ditchburn and Graham Fox, eds., *The Harper Factor: Assessing a Prime Minister's Policy Legacy* (Kingston–Montreal: McGill–Queen's University Press, 2016), 152.

18. "Harper Unveils Controversial Tax Relief for Canadian Families," *Global*

News, October 30, 2014, https://globalnews.ca/news/1645340/harper-unveils-controversial-tax-relief-for-canadian-families/.

19. Wells, *The Longer I'm Prime Minister*, 58–59.

20. Department of Finance, "Harper Government Introduces Legislation to Put More Money in the Pockets of Parents," *Government of Canada*, March 27, 2015, https://www.canada.ca/en/news/archive/2015/03/harper-government-introduces-legislation-put-more-money-pockets-parents.html.

21. Tasha Kheiriddin, "Law and Order in the Harper Years," in *The Harper Factor: Assessing a Prime Minister's Policy Legacy*, 198–199.

22. "Supreme Court Strikes Down Parole Wait Period Provision for Multiple Murderers," *CityNews Everywhere*, May 27, 2022, https://ottawa.citynews.ca/local-news/supreme-court-strikes-down-parole-wait-period-provision-for-multiple-murderers-5416244.

23. Kheiriddin, "Law and Order in the Harper Years," 199–201. Many of these sentencing changes were subsequently undone by the courts or the Liberal government of Justin Trudeau.

24. Wells, 268–270.

25. Wells, 272–273.

26. Jennifer Ditchburn, "Government News Management and Canadian Journalism," in *The Harper Factor: Assessing a Prime Minister's Policy Legacy*, 67.

27. Ditchburn, "Government News Management and Canadian Journalism," 68–69.

28. Ditchburn, 73–76.

29. "Canada Pulls Out Of, Denounces Kyoto," *CBS News*, December 13, 2011, https://www.cbsnews.com/news/canada-pulls-out-of-denounces-kyoto-protocol/.

30. "How the First Nations Education Act Fell Apart in Matter of Months," *CBC News*, May 11, 2014, https://www.cbc.ca/news/politics/how-the-first-nations-education-act-fell-apart-in-matter-of-months-1.2639378.

31. Cynthia Esley-Esquimaux, "Stephen Harper and Indigenous Peoples," in *The Harper Factor: Assessing a Prime Minister's Policy Legacy*, 224–227.

32. "Harper Rebuffs Renewed Calls for Murdered, Missing Women Inquiry," *CBC News*, August 24, 2014, https://www.cbc.ca/news/canada/manitoba/harper-rebuffs-renewed-calls-for-murdered-missing-women-inquiry-1.2742845.

33. Devon Black, "Why Does Harper Keep Spinning Our Missing

Women Tragedy?" *The Tyee*, August 27, 2014, https://thetyee.ca/
Opinion/2014/08/27/Why-Does-Harper-Keep-Spinning-Our-Missing-
Women-Tragedy/.

34. Meagan Fitzpatrick, "Harper on Terror Arrests: Not a Time for
'Sociology,'" *CBC News*, April 25, 2013, https://www.cbc.ca/news/politics/
harper-on-terror-arrests-not-a-time-for-sociology-1.1413502.

35. Leslie MacKinnon, "Harper Slams Trudeau for Comments on Boston
Bombings," *CBC News*, April 17, 2013, https://www.cbc.ca/news/politics/
harper-slams-trudeau-for-comments-on-boston-bombings-1.1394586.

36. Meagan Fitzpatrick, "Harper on Terror Arrests: Not a Time for
'Sociology.'"

37. Dr. Steve Hewitt, "How Canada's Conservative Party Is Brazenly Playing
the Terrorism Card," *The Conversation*, August 17, 2015, https://www.
birmingham.ac.uk/research/perspective/canadas-conservative-party-
terrorism.aspx.

38. Stephanie Levitz, "Canada Not in Running for UN Security Council
Seat in 2014, *Toronto Star*, May 1, 2013, https://www.thestar.com/news/
canada/2013/05/01/canada_not_in_running_for_un_security_council_
seat_in_2014_foreign_affairs_minister_john_baird_says.html.

Chapter Two: The Trudeau Years: From Sunny Ways to Stormy Days

1. Andrew Coyne, "Liberals Fail to Grasp Direness of their Situation,
Nearly a Year After Collapse," *National Post*, April 18, 2012, https://
nationalpost.com/opinion/andrew-coyne-liberals-fail-to-grasp-direness-
of-their-situation-nearly-a-year-after-collapse.

2. "Peter C. Newman on the Death of the Liberal Party," *CBC News*,
November 19, 2011, https://www.cbc.ca/news/politics/peter-c-newman-
on-the-death-of-the-liberal-party-1.1042535. In an ironic aside, Newman
scoffed at the suggestion of an alliance with the New Democrats: "They
can't even be in the same room together." Fast forward to 2022—how
things have changed.

3. John Ibbitson and Darrell Bricker, *The Big Shift: The Seismic Change in
Canadian Politics, Business, and Culture and What It Means for Our Future*
(Toronto: HarperCollins Publishers, 2013), 1397 of 3229, Kindle.

4. Ibbitson and Bricker, 98 of 3229, Kindle.

5. Aaron Wherry, preface to *Promise and Peril: Justin Trudeau in Power*
(Toronto: HarperCollins Publishers, 2019), 6.

6. John Ivison, *Trudeau: The Education of a Prime Minister* (Toronto: Signal

Books, 2019), 3.

7. Shannon Proudfoot, "Justin Trudeau's Sunny Ways Won in 2015. Can His Brand Survive?" *Maclean's*, July 31, 2018, https://www.macleans.ca/politics/ottawa/justin-trudeaus-sunny-ways-won-in-2015-can-his-brand-survive/.

8. Catherine Hakim, *Erotic Capital: The Power of Attraction in the Boardroom and the Bedroom* (New York: Basic Books, 2011), 2. Hakim defines erotic capital as "a combination of physical and social attractiveness that makes some men and women agreeable company and colleagues, attractive to all members of their society, and especially to the opposite sex." This element, she claims, is often overlooked when assessing the appeal of candidates in business and politics but can in fact be a defining part of a candidate's success.

9. Ivison, *Trudeau*, 68–69.

10. Jeremy Nuttall, "As Aylan's Story Unfolds, A Look at Canada's Syrian Refugee Promises," *The Tyee*, September 3, 2015, https://thetyee.ca/News/2015/09/03/Canada-Syrian-Refugee-Promises/.

11. Lucas Powers, "Conservatives Pledge Funds, Tip Line to Combat 'Barbaric Cultural Practices,'" *CBC News*, October 2, 2015, https://www.cbc.ca/news/politics/canada-election-2015-barbaric-cultural-practices-law-1.3254118.

12. Hannah Thibedeau and John Paul Tasker, "Conservative Post-Election Report Says O'Toole Was 'Over-Managed' During the Campaign," *CBC News*, January 27, 2022, https://www.cbc.ca/news/politics/otoole-post-election-report-1.6329961.

13. "Chris Alexander on 'Barbaric Cultural Practices': It's Why We Lost," *CTV News*, October 9, 2016, https://www.ctvnews.ca/politics/chris-alexander-on-barbaric-cultural-practices-it-s-why-we-lost-1.3106488.

14. Stephanie Taylor, "'Barbaric Cultural Practices' Hotline Idea Still Haunts Tories, MP Says," *Global News*, November 14, 2021, https://globalnews.ca/news/8373704/barbaric-cultural-practices-conservatives-2021/.

15. Daniel Lee and Maleeha Shahid, in discussion with the author, February 23, 2022.

16. Wherry, *Promise and Peril*, 12.

17. Lisa Birch and François Pétry, "Assessing Justin Trudeau's Performance at Fulfilling Campaign Pledges," in *Assessing Justin Trudeau's Liberal Government: 353 Promises and a Mandate for Change* (Quebec: Presses de l'Université Laval, 2019), 13.

18. In comparison, the researchers found Stephen Harper achieved a score of 85 percent—they did not break this down by complete of partially kept promises, however.

19. Fraser Institute, "Canadians Will Pay for Trudeau Government's Record Spending," *Toronto Sun*, April 7, 2021, https://www.fraserinstitute.org/article/canadians-will-pay-for-trudeau-governments-record-spending.

20. Fraser Institute, "Canadians Will Pay for Trudeau Government's Record Spending."

21. Marcelin Joanis and Stéphanie Lapierre, "Economic Policies: Did the Liberals Strengthen the Middle Class?" in *Assessing Justin Trudeau's Liberal Government*, 77. In fact, Trudeau broke all four of his main economic promises, including his promise to reduce the nation's debt-to-GDP ratio to 27 percent in his first term.

22. Justin Trudeau (@JustinTrudeau), "As Prime Minister, I'll make sure the 2015 election will be the last under first-past-the-post system lpc.ca/ao3o #upfordebate," Twitter, September 21, 2015, 8:09 p.m., https://twitter.com/justintrudeau/status/646114034463338497?lang=en.

23. Ivison, 172.

24. Thierry Rodon and Martin Papillon, "Renewing the Relationship with Indigenous Peoples: An Ambitious Discourse, Limited Accomplishments," in *Assessing Justin Trudeau's Liberal Government*, 179.

25. "Feds Remain Committed to Ending Boil Water Advisories, Trudeau Tells AFN," *Global News*, December 9, 2021, https://globalnews.ca/news/8438405/trudeau-first-nations-water-advisories/.

26. Mario Swampy and Kerry Black, "Tip of the Iceberg: The True State of Drinking Water Advisories in First Nations," *UCalgary News*, May 7, 2021, https://ucalgary.ca/news/tip-iceberg-true-state-drinking-water-advisories-first-nations.

27. "Indigenous Children Set to Receive Billions After Judge Rejects Trudeau Challenges," *The Guardian*, September 29, 2021, https://www.theguardian.com/global-development/2021/sep/29/canada-indigenous-children-first-nations-trudeau.

28. Catherine Porter and Vjosa Isai, "Canada Pledges $31.5 Billion to Settle Fight Over Indigenous Welfare System," *The New York Times*, January 4, 2022, https://www.nytimes.com/2022/01/04/world/canada/canada-indigenous-children-settlement.html.

29. Kathleen Harris, "Justin Trudeau Gives Provinces until 2018 to Adopt Carbon Price Plan," *CBC News*, October 3, 2016, https://www.cbc.ca/news/politics/canada-trudeau-climate-change-1.3788825.

30. Kathleen Harris, "Justin Trudeau Gives Provinces until 2018 to Adopt Carbon Price Plan."

31. Steven Chase, Kelly Cryderman, Jeff Lewis, "Trudeau Government to Buy Kinder Morgan's Trans Mountain for $4.5 Billion," *The Globe and*

Mail, May 29, 2018, https://www.theglobeandmail.com/politics/article-trudeau-government-to-buy-kinder-morgans-trans-mountain-pipeline/.

32. Wherry, 84.

33. With the program now indexed to inflation as of 2018, and with inflation rates rising at unprecedented and unforeseen rates, it will be interesting to see whether the government maintains indexation and how this impacts future budgets.

34. Wherry, 88.

35. Alison Dudu, Zeus Eden, Theo Iordache, and Nathan McLean, "Is the Canada Child Benefit an Effective Policy? Impacts on Earnings and Incomes," *Finances of the Nation,* October 28, 2021,

https://financesofthenation.ca/2021/10/28/is-the-canada-child-benefit-an-effective-policy-impacts-on-earnings-and-incomes/. The authors further note that overall, women worked two hundred hours fewer a year than before the CCB, while men's working hours remained unchanged.

36. Joanis and Lapierre, "Economic Policies: Did the Liberals Strengthen the Middle Class?" 82.

37. Wherry, 88.

38. Aimee Picchi, "Why the US Middle Class Is Falling Behind Canada's," *CBS News,* April 23, 2014, https://www.cbsnews.com/news/why-the-us-middle-class-is-falling-behind-canadas/.

Chapter Three: Trudeau's True Legacy: Stoking the Woke

1. "Trudeau Unveils Liberal Platform for a Strong Middle Class," The Liberal Party of Canada's website, October 5, 2015, https://liberal.ca/trudeau-unveils-liberal-platform-for-a-strong-middle-class/.

2. Franco Terrazzano and Kris Sims, "Opinion: Trudeau Government Broke the Debt Clock," *Toronto Sun,* March 27, 2022, https://torontosun.com/opinion/columnists/opinion-trudeau-government-broke-the-debt-clock.

3. Jenny Yuen, "Trudeau Leads the Pack When It Comes to Raising Debt: Fraser Institute," *Toronto Sun,* February 4, 2020, https://torontosun.com/news/national/trudeau-leads-the-pack-when-it-comes-to-raising-debt-fraser-institute.

4. "2019 Federal Election Platform Tracker: Where the Major Parties Stand So Far," *BNN Bloomberg,* October 15, 2019, https://www.bnnbloomberg.ca/2019-federal-election-platform-tracker-where-the-major-parties-stand-so-far-1.1308714#FISCAL%20PLAN.

5. "Justin Trudeau Says Anti-abortion Candidates Can't Run as Liberals," *National Post*, May 7, 2014, https://nationalpost.com/news/politics/justin-trudeau-says-anti-abortion-candidates-cant-run-as-liberals.

6. Joan Bryden, "Liberals Set to Turf Two MPs Accused of Sexual Misconduct," *The Globe and Mail*, March 18, 2015, https://www.theglobeandmail.com/news/politics/two-liberal-mps-accused-of-sexual-harassment-to-get-permanent-boot-from-caucus/article23515136/.

7. John Ivison, *Trudeau: The Education of a Prime Minister* (Toronto: Signal Books, 2019), 8.

8. Justin Trudeau (@JustinTrudeau), "We're a government committed to science and evidence-based policy, and Dr. Nemer your work is so very key to that. Thanks for the update today. [Quoted, Dr. Mona Nemer: Science is key to stronger government and more effective policies. I had an excellent discussion with PM @JustinTrudeau today about the impact of government support for research. I'm proud of the momentum we've created and look forward to the work ahead.]," Twitter, November 5, 2018, 5:49 p.m., https://twitter.com/justintrudeau/status/1059578521679486976?lang=en.

9. Cornell Belcher, "Book Excerpt: Cornell Belcher's *A Black Man in the White House*," *ABC News*, January 15, 2017, https://abcnews.go.com/Politics/book-excerpt-cornell-belchers-black-man-white-house/story?id=44788623.

10. "Professor Says Obama's Failure to Boldly Confront Racism Paved Way for Trump Presidency," *CBC Radio: As It Happens*, https://www.cbc.ca/radio/asithappens/as-it-happens-wednesday-edition-1.3941076/professor-says-obama-s-failure-to-boldly-confront-racism-paved-way-for-trump-presidency-1.3941539.

11. Benjamin Bell, "Jimmy Carter Says Obama's Election Inflamed Some Racists," *ABC News*, July 12, 2015, https://abcnews.go.com/Politics/jimmy-carter-president-obamas-election-inflamed-racists/story?id=32391871.

12. Ivison, *Trudeau*, 141.

13. "Woman Behind Trudeau Groping Allegations Stands by Account," *BBC News*, July 7, 2018, https://www.bbc.com/news/world-us-canada-44746886.

14. Wherry, 276.

15. Jim Bronskill, Colin Perkel, and Liam Casey, "Trudeau Takes a Knee at Anti-racism Demonstration," *CTV News*, June 5, 2020, https://www.ctvnews.ca/canada/trudeau-takes-a-knee-at-anti-racism-demonstration-1.4970650.

16. Jonathan Bradley, "Trudeau Accused of 'Humiliating' RCMP by Kneeling at Anti-racism Protest, Former Police Officer Says," *National Post*, July 7, 2020, https://nationalpost.com/news/0708-na-knee.

17. Dave Naylor, "Trudeau Calls the Unvaccinated Racist and Misogynistic Extremists," *Western Standard*, December 29, 2021, https://westernstandardonline.com/2021/12/trudeau-calls-the-unvaccinated-racist-and-misogynistic-extremists/.

18. Wherry, 274–275.

19. Wherry, 276.

20. Sara Fischer, "Distrust in Political, Media, and Business Leaders Sweeps the Globe," *Axios*, January 18, 2022, https://www.axios.com/2022/01/18/distrust-in-political-media-and-business-leaders-sweeps-the-globe. According to Edelman's annual trust barometer, in 2022, "A majority of people globally believe journalists (67 percent), government leaders (66 percent) and business executives (63 percent) are "purposely trying to mislead people by saying things they know are false or gross exaggerations."

21. Susan Delacourt, "Look Out Conservatives—Big Government Is Back, and Canadians Like It," *Toronto Star*, March 29, 2022, https://www.thestar.com/politics/political-opinion/2022/03/29/look-out-conservatives-big-government-is-back-and-canadians-like-it.html.

22. "NP View: COVID-Income Supports Must End for the Recovery to Truly Begin," *National Post*, October 8, 2021, https://nationalpost.com/opinion/np-view-covid-income-supports-must-end-for-the-recovery-to-truly-begin.

23. Jamie Watt, "An Election 'About Nothing'? Far From It—The Last Six Weeks Fundamentally Changed the Political Dynamic and Our Expectations," *Toronto Star*, September 26, 2021, https://www.thestar.com/opinion/contributors/2021/09/26/an-election-about-nothing-far-from-it-the-last-six-weeks-fundamentally-changed-the-political-dynamic-and-our-expectations.html.

24. Brett Bundale, "Rich Get Richer, Poor Poorer: Two Reports Say Pandemic Intensifying Inequalities," *CTV News*, October 13, 2020, https://www.ctvnews.ca/business/rich-get-richer-poor-poorer-two-reports-say-pandemic-intensifying-inequalities-1.5142835.

25. Joel Kotkin, "The Working Classes Are a Volcano Waiting to Erupt," *National Post*, April 24, 2022, https://nationalpost.com/news/joel-kotkin-the-working-classes-are-a-volcano-waiting-to-erupt.

26. Cassandra Drudi, "Canada's Housing Market Is Breaking Records at an Alarming Rate," *Pivot Magazine*, February 16, 2022, https://

www.cpacanada.ca/en/news/pivot-magazine/2022-02-16-housing-market#:~:text=Overall%2C%20the%20national%20MLS%20Home,per%20cent%20from%20November%202020. The national MLS→ Home Price Index increased by 25.3 percent between 2020 and 2021.

27. Ari Altstedter, "Investors Own Nearly a Third of Homes in Major Canadian Markets," *BNN Bloomberg*, April 12, 2022, https://www.bnnbloomberg.ca/investors-own-nearly-a-third-of-homes-in-major-canadian-markets-1.1751364.

28. Craig Lord, "Sixty-Three Percent of Canadian Non-owners Have 'Given Up' on Ever Buying a Home: Ipsos," *Global News*, April 29, 2022, https://globalnews.ca/news/8794099/canada-real-estate-giving-up-owning-home/.

29. Jessica Owen, "Province Flip-Flops on Extended Winter School Breaks, Causing Frustration," *Barrie Today*, November 18, 2020, https://www.barrietoday.com/coronavirus-covid-19-local-news/province-flip-flops-on-extended-winter-school-breaks-causing-frustration-2889398.

30. Polling by Discover for Navigator done in January 2022 found that only 29 percent of Albertans felt confident about their provincial government's plan to deal with the pandemic, versus 61 percent in Quebec, 55 percent in Atlantic Canada and 51 percent in BC. In Manitoba and Saskatchewan, 39 percent felt confident, whereas in Ontario, it was 36 percent. Similarly, when it came to confidence in Prime Minister Trudeau's plan, 34 percent of Albertans were confident, versus 60 percent in Quebec, 55 percent in Atlantic Canada, 46 percent in BC, 43 percent in Ontario and 38 percent in Manitoba–Saskatchewan.

31. Pierre Poilievre (@PierrePoilievre), "Money-printing deficits make our wages 'go up in smoke'. #JustinFlation We need sound money again—and also the freedom for buyers and sellers to choose #bitcoin and other technology. Become a member, so you can vote: [Quoted, YouTube: Wages go up in smoke]," Twitter, April 1, 2022, 11:29 a.m., https://twitter.com/PierrePoilievre/status/1509915860160303112.

32. Pierre Poilievre (@PierrePoilievre), "The COVID control freaks are never satisfied. Now they want to push to mandate a third dose. End vaccine mandates. All of them. Now. [Quoted, *CTV News*: It's 'high time' that authorities revise definitions of 'fully vaccinated': experts]," Twitter, June 6, 2022, 10:17 a.m., https://twitter.com/PierrePoilievre/status/1533815378908000257.

33. Brian Lilley, "Charest Says Poilievre's Support for Trucker Convoy Disqualifies Him from Leadership," *Toronto Sun*, April 11, 2022, https://torontosun.com/news/national/charest-says-poilievres-support-for-trucker-convoy-disqualifies-him-from-leadership.

Chapter Four: Populism in Canada: Everything Old is New Again

1. Stephen J. Harper. *Right Here, Right Now: Politics and Leadership in the Age of Disruption* (Toronto: Signal Books, 2018), 43.

2. Stephen J. Harper, *Right Here, Right Now*, 48.

3. Stephen J. Harper, 77.

4. Provincially, it had more success; its Ontario version, the United Farmers of Ontario, won the general election there in 1919. More Progressive MPs were elected in Ontario in the 1921 election than in any other province, challenging the notion that this was a "Western protest party."

5. J. T. Morley, "Social Credit," *The Canadian Encyclopedia*, May 28, 2018, https://www.thecanadianencyclopedia.ca/en/article/social-credit.

6. Lewis Thomas, ed., *William Aberhart and Social Credit in Alberta* (Toronto: Copp Clark Publishing, 1977), 67–69.

7. Preston Manning, *Do Something!: 365 Ways You Can Strengthen Canada* (Toronto: Sutherland House, 2020), 19–20.

8. Manning, *Do Something!*, 21.

9. Tasha Kheiriddin and Adam Daifallah, *Rescuing Canada's Right: Blueprint for a Conservative Revolution* (Toronto: Wiley, 2005), 23.

10. Plamondon, *Blue Thunder*, 225.

11. Blair Fraser, "Can Diefenbaker Fulfill His Election Promises?" *Maclean's*, August 31, 1957, https://archive.macleans.ca/article/1957/8/31/can-diefenbaker-fulfill-his-election-promises.

12. John Meisel, *The Canadian General Election of 1957*, (Toronto: University of Toronto Press, 1962), 286.

13. "John Diefenbaker and the Canadian Bill of Rights," *CBC Archives*, accessed November 5, 2021, https://www.cbc.ca/player/play/1771116001.

14. Bobby Hristova, "Rise in People's Party Support 'Very Concerning' Even If Its Future Is Concerning, Expert Says," *CBC News*, September 21, 2021, https://www.cbc.ca/news/canada/hamilton/ppc-results-1.6183876.

15. Rachel Pannett, "Who Is Maxime Bernier? The Far-Right Politician Compared to Trump Could Help Trudeau in Canada's Next Election," *Washington Post*, September 13, 2021, https://www.washingtonpost.com/world/2021/09/13/canada-election-conservative-ppc-maxime-bernier/.

16. Christy Somos, "What the Rise of the PPC Says About Canada in 2021," *CTV News*, September 22, 2021, https://www.ctvnews.ca/politics/federal-

election-2021/what-the-rise-of-the-ppc-says-about-canada-in-2021-1.5596859?cache=%3FcontactForm%3Dtrue.

17. Maxime Bernier (@MaximeBernier), "1/2 Pierre Poilievre keeps lying about opposing vaccine mandates 'from day one.' Proof: After the election, O'Toole excluded seven MPs from his shadow cabinet who had spoken out against these mandates, but PP was reinstated as finance critic. [Quoted, *CBC News*: O'Toole Leaves MPs Who Questioned Vaccine Policy Out of His Shadow Cabinet]," Twitter, May 31, 2022, 9:09 a.m., https://twitter.com/MaximeBernier/status/1531623955253141504?ref_src=twsrc%5Egoogle%7Ctwcamp%5Eserp%7Ctwgr%5Etweet.

18. Ian Brown, "They Came. They Idled. They Left. What Have Convoy Protesters Been Doing Since They Went Home?" *The Globe and Mail*, June 4, 2022, https://www.theglobeandmail.com/canada/article-ottawa-convoy-protesters-visit-at-home/.

19. Leslyn Lewis's website, ""World Health Assembly Vote: Conspiracy or Fact?" https://leslynlewis.ca/blog/world-health-assembly-vote-conspiracy-or-fact/.

20. Leslyn Lewis Campaign Updates, email message to author, June 1, 2022.

21. Sean Davidson, "Ontario MP Kicked Out of PC Caucus for Calling Lockdown 'Deadlier Than Covid,'" *CTV News*, January 15, 2021, https://toronto.ctvnews.ca/ontario-mpp-kicked-out-of-pc-caucus-for-calling-lockdown-deadlier-than-covid-1.5268225.

22. Roman Baber (@Roman_Baber), "Public Health & the 'experts' are blaming Delta instead of admitting they were wrong or worse, they lied about the longevity of the vaccine. We were told the vaccine was our ticket out but 6 months later we need a booster? Why trust Public Health? [Quoted, *Reuters*: U.S. Plans COVID-19 Booster Shots at Six Months Instead of Eight—WSJ]," Twitter, August 30, 2021, 7:23 a.m., https://twitter.com/roman_baber/status/1432303016896516100?lang=ar.

23. Pierre Poilievre (@PierrePoilievre), "The globalist World Economic Forum—which Trudeau, Freeland & Carney so adore says, 'You'll Own Nothing. And You'll Be Happy.' Maybe that's why government is inflating home prices," Twitter, July 17, 2021, 8:30 a.m., https://twitter.com/pierrepoilievre/status/1416374627748696065.

24. Pierre Poilievre (@PierrePoilievre), "The COVID control freaks are never satisfied. Now they want to push to mandate a third dose. End vaccine mandates. All of them. Now."

25. Wells, 314.

26. Paul Wells, "Pierre Poilievre, moderate: Audit the Bank of Canada? Uh... sure?" Paul Wells (Substack), April 29, 2022, https://paulwells.substack.com/p/pierre-poilievre-moderate?s=r.

27. "An Inside Look at Patrick Brown's Pitch for Selling Conservative Party Memberships," *CTV News*, April 18, 2022, https://toronto.ctvnews.ca/an-inside-look-at-patrick-brown-s-pitch-for-selling-conservative-party-memberships-1.5865275.

28. James Wellstead, "Canadian Wheat Board Dismantled," *Investing News Network*, October 20, 2011, https://investingnews.com/daily/resource-investing/agriculture-investing/potash-investing/canadian-wheat-board-dismantled/.

29. Melanie Risdon, "Bernier Says Poilievre Is 'Leftist' on Supply Management Issue," *Western Standard*, March 16, 2022, https://westernstandardonline.com/2022/03/bernier-says-poilievre-is-leftist-on-supply-management-issue/.

Chapter Five: Conservatism in Canada: Building the Big Tent

1. Drea Humphrey (@DreaHumphrey), "'I feel like I'm being shouted at by a CBC journalist or something' joked CPC leadership candidate Pierre Poilievre before promising to 'save a billion dollars by defunding the CBC' if elected Prime Minister. Reports on the race at LeadershipReports.ca," Twitter, April 8, 2022, 12:06 p.m., https://twitter.com/DreaHumphrey/status/1512492551357431811; Pierre Poilievre, "Speech on Freedom," April 8, 2022, Croatian Cultural Centre, Vancouver, BC.

2. Edmund Burke, "Reflections on the Revolution in France, (1790)," *The Works of the Right Honourable Edmund Burke*, vol. 3 (1899), 359.

3. Roger Scruton, *How to Be a Conservative*, reprinted ed. (New York: Bloomsbury Continuum, 2015), 20.

4. Scruton, *How to Be a Conservative*, 8–9.

5. Edmund Burke, "Reflections on the Revolution in France."

6. George Grant, *Lament for a Nation: The Defeat of Canadian Nationalism*, 40th Anniversary ed. (Kingston: McGill–Queen's University Press, 2005) 63–64.

7. Grant, *Lament for a Nation*, 67.

8. Mario Canseco, "Religious Adherence Differs Greatly in Canada and United States," *Research Co.*, December 15, 2020, https://researchco.ca/2020/12/15/religion-canada-usa/.

9. Canseco, "Religious Adherence Differs Greatly in Canada and United States."

10. Kheiriddin and Daifallah, *Rescuing Canada's Right.*

11. Kheiriddin and Daifallah, 62.

12. Kheiriddin and Daifallah, 62.

13. William Watson, "The Budget That Changed Canada," *Financial Post*, February 27, 2020, https://financialpost.com/opinion/william-watson-the-budget-that-changed-canada.

14. "Bernard Drainville, "Father of Quebec Values Charter, Trying Politics Again, This Time with CAQ," *CBC News*, June 3, 2022, https://www.cbc.ca/news/canada/montreal/bernard-drainville-caq-1.6476751.

15. Eric Andrew-Gee, "Quebec By-election a Sign of Existential Danger for the Storied Parti Québécois," *The Globe and Mail*, April 13, 2022, https://www.theglobeandmail.com/canada/article-quebec-by-election-a-sign-of-existential-danger-for-the-storied-parti/.

16. Hugh Segal, *Beyond Greed: A Traditional Conservative Confronts Neoconservative Excess* (Toronto: Stoddart Publishing, 1997), 164.

17. Segal, *Beyond Greed,* 165–166.

18. Grant, 63–64.

19. "Conservative Constitution," *The Conservative Party of Canada*, August 25, 2018, https://cpcassets.conservative.ca/wp-content/uploads/2020/10/13160144/98161775845df04.pdf.

Chapter Six: Opportunity Knocks! Will Conservatives Answer?

1. A supply-and-confidence motion is one whereby a party or independent members of Parliament agree to support the government in motions of confidence and appropriation or budget (supply) votes, so as not to bring down the government.

2. Amanda Connolly and Ahmar Khan, "Trudeau Confirms Liberals, NDP Governance Deal until 2025," *Global News*, March 22, 2022, https://globalnews.ca/news/8700158/trudeau-singh-liberals-ndp-tentative-deal/.

3. Mitch Heimpel, "So Long, Business Liberals," *The Line*, June 7, 2022, https://theline.substack.com/p/mitch-heimpel-so-long-business-liberals?s=r.

4. Steve Burgess, "Abortion. Bitcoin. Political Orphans. That Was Some

Debate," *The Tyee*, May 12, 2022, https://thetyee.ca/Analysis/2022/05/12/Conservative-Leadership-Debate/.

5. Stephanie Levitz, "'Who Speaks for the Centre?' A New Group of Conservatives Says the Party's Path to Victory Is Right Down the Middle," *Toronto Star*, April 20, 2022, https://www.thestar.com/politics/federal/2022/04/20/who-speaks-for-the-centre-a-new-group-of-conservatives-says-the-partys-path-to-victory-is-right-down-the-middle.html.

6. Rick Peterson, email message to author, May 17, 2022.

7. Chantal Da Silva, "'I Just Don't Feel Safe': Ottawa Residents Describe Fears Amid Trucker Protest As Canada's Far Right Comes into Focus," *NBC News*, February 10, 2022, https://www.nbcnews.com/news/-just-dont-feel-safe-ottawa-residents-describe-fears-trucker-protest-c-rcna15218.

8. Joe Castaldo, "Border Blockade Damaged Canada's Reputation, Business Leaders Say," *The Globe and Mail*, February 14, 2022, https://www.theglobeandmail.com/business/article-industry-groups-concerned-border-blockade-has-damaged-canadas/.

9. Philippe J. Fournier, "338Canada: Why Canada's Conservatives Are Choking on Diesel Fumes," *Politico*, May 11, 2022, https://www.politico.com/news/2022/05/11/338canada-canada-conservatives-convoy-protest-00031535.

10. Kheiriddin and Daifallah, 193.

11. Brian Lee Crowley, *A Modern Conservatism for a Modern Canada: An MLI Collection of Essays* (Ottawa: Macdonald–Laurier Institute, 2022), https://macdonaldlaurier.ca/wp-content/uploads/2022/04/Apr2022_A_Modern_Conservatism_for_a_Modern_Canada_BLC_COLLECTION_FWeb.pdf?mc_cid=d755606b8e&mc_eid=c92f403a55, 14.

12. Crowley, *A Modern Conservatism for a Modern Canada*, 25.

13. Stuart M. Butler and Matthew Spalding, "Opportunity Conservatism," *The Heritage Foundation*, May 6, 2013, https://www.heritage.org/political-process/commentary/opportunity-conservatism.

14. Ted Cruz, "GOP Needs Message of Opportunity Conservatism," *Washington Post*, January 3, 2013, https://www.washingtonpost.com/opinions/ted-cruz-gop-needs-message-of-opportunity-conservatism/2013/01/03/c9536c8e-550e-11e2-8b9e-dd8773594efc_story.html.

15. Heath Mayo, "Opportunity Conservatism: A Blueprint for a Post-Trump GOP," *Medium*, October 9, 2018, https://medium.com/@HeathMayo/

opportunity-conservatism-a-blueprint-for-a-post-trump-gop-6d0dc65b010d.

16. Eric S. M. Protzer, "Social Mobility Explains Populism, Not Inequality or Culture," CID Research Fellow and Graduate Student Working Paper No. 118 (September 2019), Centre for International Development at Harvard University, https://www.hks.harvard.edu/centers/cid/publications/fellow-graduate-student-working-papers/social-mobility-populism.

17. Protzer, "Social Mobility Explains Populism, Not Inequality or Culture."

18. Kotkin, "The Working Classes Are a Volcano Waiting to Erupt."

19. Kotkin, "The Working Classes Are a Volcano Waiting to Erupt."

20. Eric Protzer and Paul Summerville, *Reclaiming Populism: How Economic Fairness Can Win Back Disenchanted Voters* (Cambridge: Polity Press, 2022), 92.

21. Christopher Nardi, "Elections Canada Chief Concerned About Increased Violence Towards Poll Workers," *National Post*, May 7, 2022, https://nationalpost.com/news/politics/elections-canada-chief-concerned-about-increased-violence-towards-poll-workers.

22. "Transcript: The Populist Challenge," *TVO Today*, February 23, 2022, https://www.tvo.org/transcript/2688661/the-populist-challenge.

23. Lucas F. Stoetzer, "How Does Income Inequality Affect Support for Populist Parties?" *The London School of Economics and Political Science*, November 11, 2021, https://blogs.lse.ac.uk/europpblog/2021/11/11/how-does-income-inequality-affect-support-for-populist-parties/.

24. Laura Brogi, *Intergenerational Mobility and the Rise of Populism* (Belgium: Parienté, William, 2019), Faculté des sciences économiques, sociales, politiques, et de communication, Université catholique de Louvain, https://dial.uclouvain.be/downloader/downloader.php?pid=thesis%3A177 82&datastream=PDF_01&cover=cover-mem, 18.

25. Stephanie Taylor, "Preston Manning Says Populism Out of COVID Trucker Convoy Must Be 'Properly Managed,'" *National Newswatch*, May 6, 2022, https://www.nationalnewswatch.com/2022/05/06/bergen-says-conservatives-wont-attract-disaffected-liberals-by-being-liberal-lite/#.YnWjN-jMK5d.

26. "Freedom Index by Country 2022," World Population Review, https://worldpopulationreview.com/country-rankings/freedom-index-by-country.

27. Protzer and Summerville, *Reclaiming Populism*, 99.

28. Protzer and Summerville, 99.

29. Edmund Burke, *Complete Works of Edmund Burke*, illustrated ed. (East Sussex: Delphi Classics, 2016), 1426.

Chapter Seven: Immigration Nation: The New Canadian Vote

1. John Ibbitson, "The Politics of 2036, When Canada Is as Brown as It Is White," *The Globe and Mail*, January 27, 2017, https://www.theglobeandmail.com/news/politics/the-politics-of-2036-when-canada-is-as-brown-as-it-is-white/article33814437/.

2. Immigration, Refugees, and Citizenship Canada, "New Immigration Plan to Fill Labour Market Shortages and Grow Canada's Economy," *Government of Canada*, February 14, 2022, https://www.canada.ca/en/immigration-refugees-citizenship/news/2022/02/new-immigration-plan-to-fill-labour-market-shortages-and-grow-canadas-economy.html.

3. *Century Initiative*, https://www.centuryinitiative.ca/.

4. Crowley, 7.

5. "'I Don't Know What It Means to Fly the Canadian Flag Anymore.' Protests and the Maple Leaf, Plus Other Letters to the Editor," *The Globe and Mail*, February 19, 2022, https://www.theglobeandmail.com/opinion/letters/article-feb-19-i-dont-know-what-it-means-to-fly-the-canadian-flag-any-more/.

6. Scruton, 91.

7. Brian Mulroney, in discussion with the author, October 30, 2021.

8. Mulroney, in discussion with the author.

9. John Ibbitson, "Conservatives Changed the Nature of Canadian Immigration, *The Globe and Mail*, December 16, 2014, https://www.theglobeandmail.com/news/politics/how-conservatives-changed-the-nature-of-canadian-immigration/article22101709/.

10. John Paul Tasker, "After Monday's Vote, the Federal Conservative Caucus Will Be 95 Per Cent White," *CBC News*, September 22, 2021, https://www.cbc.ca/news/politics/conserative-caucus-95-per-cent-white-1.6185707.

11. Mark Gollom, "Stephen Harper's 'Old-Stock Canadians': Politics of Division or Simple Slip?" *CBC News*, September 19, 2015, https://www.cbc.ca/news/politics/old-stock-canadians-stephen-harper-identity-politics-1.3234386. In his 2015 campaign, Harper was criticized for using the term "old-stock Canadians" to describe Canadians whose families stretched back several generations, in contrast to those of newcomers. The term is considered a "dog-whistle."

12. "Longitudinal Immigration Database: Immigrant and Census Metropolitan Area Tables, 2018," *Statistics Canada*, March 22, 2021, https://www150.statcan.gc.ca/n1/daily-quotidien/210322/dq210322c-eng.htm.

13. Walied Soliman, in discussion with the author, May 19, 2022.

14. Arjun* (a pseudonym requested by the subject), in discussion with the author, June 1, 2022, Toronto, ON.

15. Matthijs de Blois, "The True Spirit of Toleration: Edmund Burke on Establishment and Tolerance," *Netherlands Journal of Legal Philosophy* 3 (2008), https://www.elevenjournals.com/tijdschrift/rechtsfilosofieentheorie/2008/3/RenR_2008_038_003_002.pdf, 12.

16. De Blois, "The True Spirit of Toleration: Edmund Burke on Establishment and Tolerance," 12.

17. Ashleigh Stewart, "'Gone by 2040': Why Some Religions Are Declining in Canada Faster Than Ever," *Global News*, January 8, 2022, https://globalnews.ca/news/8471086/religion-decline-canada/#:~:text=Religiosity%20in%20Canada%20is%20at,tracking%20the%20data%20in%201985.

18. Ibbitson, "Conservatives Changed the Nature of Canadian Immigration."

19. Daniel Otis, "'Super Visa' Allows Some People to Stay in Canada for up to Seven Years, Here's Who Is Eligible to Apply," *CTV News*, June 7, 2022, https://www.ctvnews.ca/canada/super-visa-allows-some-people-to-stay-in-canada-for-up-to-7-years-here-s-who-is-eligible-to-apply-1.5936961.

20. "Worldwide Tax Summaries: France," *PricewaterhouseCoopers*, February 14, 2022, https://taxsummaries.pwc.com/france/individual/taxes-on-personal-income#:~:text=Under%20income%2Dsplitting%20rules%2C%20total,third%20and%20each%20subsequent%20child.

21. Sharon M. Lee and Barry Edmonston, "Canada's Immigrant Families: Growth, Diversity, and Challenges," *Population Change and Lifecourse Strategic Knowledge Cluster Discussion Paper Series* 1, no. 1 (March 2013), https://ir.lib.uwo.ca/cgi/viewcontent.cgi?article=1003&context=pclc.

22. Steven Chase, "CSIS Had Warned Government of Potential for Violence, Foreign Interference in 2021 Federal Election, *The Globe and Mail*, May 6, 2022, FIRhttps://www.theglobeandmail.com/politics/article-extremists-planned-to-commit-violence-during-2021-canadian-federal/.

23. Terry Glavin, "China's Interference in Canada's Election Doesn't Seem to Faze the Liberals," *Ottawa Citizen*, September 15, 2021, https://ottawacitizen.com/news/politics/election-2021/glavin-chinas-interference-in-canadas-election-doesnt-seem-to-faze-the-liberals.

24. Tom Blackwell, "Defeated Conservative MP Fears Attacks by Pro-Beijing Forces Swung Votes Against Him, *National Post*, September 21, 2021, https://nationalpost.com/news/politics/election-2021/defeated-tory-mp-fears-attacks-by-pro-beijing-forces-swung-votes-against-him.

25. Yuen Pao Woo, "Election Disinformation Claims and Kenny Chiu's Richmond Riding," *Policy Options*, January 31, 2022, https://policyoptions. irpp.org/magazines/january-2022/election-disinformation-claims-and-kenny-chius-richmond-riding/.

26. "Australia's New Foreign Influence Laws: Who Is Targeted?" https://www. lowyinstitute.org/the-interpreter/australia-new-foreign-influence-laws-who-targeted.

27. Sam Cooper, *Wilful Blindness: How a Criminal Network of Narcos, Tycoons and Chinese Communist Party Agents Infiltrated the West* (Toronto: Optimum Publishing International, 2021); Douglas Todd, "Sam Cooper's Exposé of Corruption in Canada Tops Bestseller List," *Vancouver Sun*, June 18, 2021, https://vancouversun.com/opinion/columnists/douglas-todd-sam-coopers-expose-of-corruption-in-canada-tops-bestseller-list.

28. Janet E. Silver, "Chinese-Canadian Voters Swing Results in Usually Tory Ridings," *iPolitics*, September 23, 2021, https://ipolitics.ca/news/chinese-canadian-voters-swing-results-in-usually-tory-ridings.

29. Jeremy Nuttall, "Canadian Lawmaker Launches Second Try for a Foreign Influence Registry," *Toronto Star*, April 1, 2022, https://www.thestar.com/news/canada/2022/04/01/canadian-lawmaker-launches-second-try-for-a-foreign-influence-registry.html.

Chapter Eight: A Country of Cities: The Urban Vote

1. Wells, *Right Side Up*, 214.

2. Jess Goddard, in discussion with the author, May 21, 2022.

3. Tanu Chopra, in discussion with the author, May 21, 2022.

4. Chopra, in discussion with the author.

5. Wells, 213–214.

6. Maleeha Shahid, in discussion with the author, May 24, 2022.

7. Shahid, in discussion with the author.

8. Shahid.

9. "Our Halton 2018 Newcomers," *Community Development Halton*, December 2018, https://cdhalton.ca/wp-content/uploads/2018/09/Our-Halton-2018-Newcomers.pdf.

10. Mike Ras, in discussion with the author, May 24, 2022.

11. Ras, in discussion with the author.

12. Ras.

13. Dave Armstrong, Jack Lucas, and Zack Taylor, "The Urban–Rural Divide in Canadian Federal Elections, 1896–2019," *Canadian Journal of Political Science* 55, no. 1 (March 2022): 84–106, https://doi.org/10.1017/S0008423921000792.

14. Armstrong, Lucas, and Taylor, "The Urban–Rural Divide in Canadian Federal Elections, 1896–2019."

15. Armstrong, Lucas, and Taylor.

16. Wells, 12.

17. Armstrong, Lucas, and Taylor.

18. Jason Roy, Andrea M.L. Perrella, and Joshua Borden, "Rural, Suburban, and Urban Voters: Dissecting Residence Based Voter Cleavages in Provincial Elections," *Canadian Political Science Review* 9, no. 1 (2015): 112–127, https://ojs.unbc.ca/index.php/cpsr/article/viewFile/1203/1007.

19. Armstrong, Lucas, and Taylor.

20. Aaron Wherry, "Two New Solitudes—Rural and Urban—Now Define the Canadian Landscape," *CBC News*, October 3, 2021, https://www.cbc.ca/news/politics/2021-election-rural-urban-conservative-liberal-1.6197095.

21. Armstrong, Lucas, and Taylor.

22. "Billions in Money Laundering Increased BC Housing Prices, Expert Panel Finds," *BC Gov News*, May 9, 2019, https://news.gov.bc.ca/releases/2019FIN0051-000914#. According to a BC government report, the laundering of $7 billion in illegal funds increased house prices by 5 percent.

23. Chris Hall, "The Trudeau Government Isn't Using All the Tools to Protect Canadians from Inflation, Economist Says," *CBC News*, May 21, 2022, https://www.cbc.ca/radio/thehouse/inflation-trudeau-freeland-1.6461208.

24. "Cross Border Abortion Rights," *Maru Public Opinion*, May 12, 2022, https://static1.squarespace.com/static/5a17333eb0786935ac112523/t/627d5f53c38f375f1dee9287/1652383572316/Abortion+Poll+F+2022+05+22.pdf.

25. Marieke Walsh and Safiyah Marhnouj, "Trudeau Renews Pledge to Protect Abortion Rights in Canada, But Unable to Offer Timeline," *The Globe and Mail*, May 4, 2022, https://www.theglobeandmail.com/politics/article-canada-abortion-rights-trudeau/.

26. "Overturning Roe v. Wade," *Leger*, May 11, 2022, https://leger360.com/surveys/legers-north-american-tracker-may-11-2022/.

27. "Cross Border Abortion Rights."

28. Kheiriddin, 197.

29. "Emergencies Act Review: Canadians Divided Whether 'Freedom Convoy' Could Have Been Dispersed Without It," *Angus Reid Institute*, May 12, 2022, https://angusreid.org/emergency-act-review-freedom-convoy/.

30. "Employer Frustrated at Canadian Who 'Just Don't Want to Work,'" *BNN Bloomberg*, June 29, 2021, https://www.bnnbloomberg.ca/employer-frustrated-at-canadians-who-just-don-t-want-to-work-1.1623217.

31. Robert Arnason, "A Prairie Labour Shortage," *The Western Producer*, November 18, 2021, https://www.producer.com/news/a-prairie-labour-shortage/.

32. "COVID-Income Supports Must End for the Recovery to Truly Begin," *National Post*, October 8, 2021, https://nationalpost.com/opinion/np-view-covid-income-supports-must-end-for-the-recovery-to-truly-begin.

33. Dustin Cook, "Alberta NDP-Connected Group Sought to Influence Edmonton's Municipal Election by Limiting Number of Progressive Candidates," *Edmonton Journal*, September 7, 2021, https://edmontonjournal.com/news/local-news/alberta-ndp-connected-group-sought-to-influence-edmontons-municipal-election-by-limiting-number-of-progressive-candidates.

34. Jack Lucas, "Do 'Non-partisan' Municipal Politicians Match the Partisanship of Their Constituents?" *Urban Affairs Review* 58, no. 1: 103–128, http://jacklucas.pennyjar.ca/uaraccepted.pdf.

35. Lucas, "Do 'Non-partisan' Municipal Politicians Match the Partisanship of Their Constituents?"

36. Benjamin Shingler and Erika Morris, "Boosting Montreal's Dismal Election Turnout Won't Be Easy, But There Are Remedies Available," *CBC News*, November 9, 2021, https://www.cbc.ca/news/canada/montreal/montreal-voter-turnout-plante-projet-montreal-1.6241569.

37. Timon Johnson, "Turnout for Alberta's Municipal Elections Weak Across the Province," *The Globe and Mail*, October 22, 2021, https://www.theglobeandmail.com/canada/alberta/article-turnout-for-albertas-municipal-elections-was-weak-across-the-province/.

Chapter Nine: Courting Young Canadians: Millennials and Gen-Z

1. "A Generational Portrait of Canada's Aging Population from the 2021 Census," *Statistics Canada*, April 27, 2022, https://www12.statcan.gc.ca/census-recensement/2021/as-sa/98-200-X/2021003/98-200-X2021003-eng.cfm.

2. "A Generational Portrait of Canada's Aging Population from the 2021 Census."

3. "A Generational Portrait of Canada's Aging Population from the 2021 Census."

4. "A Generational Portrait of Canada's Aging Population from the 2021 Census."

5. "Canadian Youth—A Social Values Perspective on Identity, Life Aspirations and Engagement of Millennials and Gen Z: Final Report" *The Environics Institute for Survey Research*, March 2022.

6. "A Generational Portrait of Canada's Aging Population from the 2021 Census."

7. Robert A. George, foreword to *GOP GPS: How to Find the Millennials and Urban Voters the Republican Party Needs to Survive*, by Evan Siegfried (New York: Skyhorse Publishing, 2016), 11.

8. Ilona Dougherty, in discussion with the author, May 25, 2022.

9. Dougherty, in discussion with the author.

10. Katie Dangerfield, "Millennials vs. Baby Boomers: Why the Cost of Living Has Skyrocketed for Young Canadians," *Global News*, June 26, 2021, https://globalnews.ca/news/7941437/millenial-housing-costs-baby-boomers/.

11. "Striving for Balance, Advocating for Change: The Deloitte Global 2022 Gen Z & Millennial Survey," *Deloitte*, 2022, https://www2.deloitte.com/content/dam/Deloitte/global/Documents/deloitte-2022-genz-millennial-survey.pdf.

12. "Generation Z in Canada," in *The Canadian Encyclopedia*, https://www.thecanadianencyclopedia.ca/en/article/generation-z-in-canada.

13. Brian Platt, "Trudeau Is Shedding Support Among 'Dislocated' Younger Voters," *Bloomberg News*, May 18, 2022, https://financialpost.com/pmn/business-pmn/trudeau-is-shedding-support-among-dislocated-younger-voters.

14. Platt, "Trudeau Is Shedding Support Among 'Dislocated' Younger Voters."

15. Éric Duhaime, in discussion with the author, May 24, 2022.

16. Goddard, in discussion with the author.

17. Tanu Chopra, email message to author, May 25, 2022.

18. Sako Khederlarian, email message to author, May 24, 2022.

19. "EKOS Research Associates Poll," *EKOS*, May 5, 2022, https://qc125.com/proj/2022-05-10-ekos.pdf.

20. "EKOS Research Associates Poll."

21. Darrell Bricker, "Nearly Half (46%) of Canadians Say They 'May not Agree with Everything' Trucker Convoy Says or Does, But . . ." *Ipsos*, February 11, 2022, htt7ps://www.ipsos.com/en-ca/news-polls/nearly-half-say-they-may-not-agree-with-trucker-convoy.

22. Brooke Auxier and Jana Arbanas, "News at Their Fingertips: Digital and Social Tech Power Gen Z Teens' News Consumption, *Deloitte Insights*, May 12, 2022, https://www2.deloitte.com/uk/en/insights/industry/technology/gen-z-news-consumption.html.

23. Aaron Moore, in discussion with the author, June 2, 2022, Toronto, ON.

24. Moore, in discussion with the author.

25. Nicole Thompson, "Doug Ford Nets Another Union Endorsement, Positions Ontario PCs as Labour Friendly," *The Globe and Mail*, May 17, 2022, https://www.theglobeandmail.com/canada/article-doug-ford-nets-another-union-endorsement-positions-ontario-pcs-as/.

26. Lesli Martin, Michael Cooper, and Brittany Saab, "Mental Health During COVID-19 Outbreak: Poll #12," *Mental Health Research Canada*, April 2022, https://static1.squarespace.com/static/5f31a311d93d0f2e28aaf04a/t/6283b264fb080c2726093d2e/1652798053575/Abridged+-+meta+tag+-+MHRC+Mental+Health+During+COVID+Poll+12+Report.pdf.

27. "Striving for Balance, Advocating for Change."

28. "Canadian Youth—A Social Values Perspective on Identity, Life Aspirations and Engagement of Millennials and Gen Z," 14.

29. "Canadian Youth—A Social Values Perspective on Identity, Life Aspirations and Engagement of Millennials and Gen Z Environics," 22

30. "Political Engagement: Generation Z: Portrait of a New Generation of Young Canadians and How They Compare to Older Canadians," *Elections Canada*, August 27, 2021, https://www.elections.ca/content.aspx?section=res&dir=rec/part/genz&document=p7&lang=e.

31. Patrick Brown, *Takedown: The Attempted Political Assassination of Patrick Brown* (Toronto: Optimum Publishing International, 2021), 27–28.

Chapter Ten: The West, the Rest, and the Best: A National Vision for National Unity

1. Monte Solberg, in discussion with the author, May 24, 2022.

2. Adam MacVicar, "Calgary MPs Weigh In on Ottawa Trucker Protest as Hope for Resolution Grows, *Global News*, February 7, 2022, https://globalnews.ca/news/8600674/calgary-mp-ottawa-trucker-protest/.

3. Stephanie Kusie (@StephanieKusie), "I'm tired of this situation being used for political gain on any side. We have a number of significant problems facing us as a nation that we need to address without the political games distracting us. Let's come together and discuss a plan for the betterment of Canada. #cdnpoli [Quoted, Candice Bergen: It is time to de-politicize the response to the pandemic and bring Canadians together again. My letter to the Prime Minister.]," Twitter, February 7, 2022, 8:36 p.m., https://twitter.com/StephanieKusie/status/1490861999873478656.

4. Blair Fraser, "Can Diefenbaker Fulfill His Election Promises?" *Maclean's*, August 31, 1957, https://archive.macleans.ca/article/1957/8/31/can-diefenbaker-fulfill-his-election-promises.

5. Solberg, in discussion with the author.

6. Leo Housakos, in discussion with the author, October 13, 2021.

7. Peter MacKay, in discussion with the author, February 20, 2022.

8. John Baird, in discussion with the author, December 3, 2021.

9. Baird, in discussion with the author.

10. MacKay, in discussion with the author.

11. Gordon Pitts, "Calgary's Corporate Radical," *Institute of Corporate Directors*, March 4, 2016, https://static1.squarespace.com/static/5b621c23f8370a2a9d28c0e9/t/5cd306cae79c70dc1378d32f/1557333707132/Calgary%27s+corporate+radical+-+%282016%29+-+ICD.pdf.

12. Mac Van Wielingen, "What Is the Future of Canada's Energy Sector?" *Emerging Themes of an Optimal Pathway," The School of Public Policy Publications: SPP Pre-publication Series* (June 2021), The School of Public Policy, University of Calgary, https://www.policyschool.ca/wp-content/uploads/2021/06/AF6_Canadas-Energy-Sector_Van-Wielingen.pdf.

13. Mac Van Wielingen, in discussion with the author, January 7, 2022.

14. Van Wielingen, in discussion with the author.

15. Jean Charest's website, "Charest Launches Plan to Drive Clean Growth and Real Environmental Results," https://www.jeancharest.ca/charest-clean-growth-and-environment/.

16. Alex Ballingall, "Demand Is Suddenly Soaring for Electric Vehicle Batteries. Can Canada Seize the Moment?" *Toronto Star*, January 20, 2022, https://www.thestar.com/politics/federal/2022/01/30/demand-is-suddenly-soaring-for-electric-vehicle-batteries-can-canada-seize-the-moment.html.

17. Christopher Barnard, "China Seeks to Extend Critical Minerals

Monopoly with Help of Taliban," *The Hill*, September 20, 2021, https://thehill.com/opinion/energy-environment/572932-china-seeks-to-extend-critical-minerals-monopoly-with-help-of/.

18. Gerry St. Germain, email message to author, June 1, 2022.

19. St. Germain, email message to author.

20. St. Germain, email message to author.

21. Van Wielingen, in discussion with the author.

Conclusion: Return of the Liberal–Conservative Party?

1. George Grant, *Lament for a Nation: The Defeat of Canadian Nationalism* (Ottawa: Carleton University Press, 1995).

2. Benjamin Disraeli, "Speech on Reform Bill of 1867," October 20, 1867, Edinburgh, Scotland; quoted in *The Life of Benjamin Disraeli, Earl of Beaconsfield* by William Flavelle Monypenny and George Earle Buckle, vol. 2 (London: John Murray, 1929), 291.

3. Benjamin Disraeli, "Campaign Speech," November 27, 1832, High Wycombe, England; quoted in *Selected Speeches of the Late Right Honourable the Earl of Beaconsfield*, ed. T. E. Kebbel, vol. 1 (1882), 8.

INDEX

Black, Kerry, 33
Blacks, political party membership, 88
Bloc Québécois, 138–39
Boebert, Lauren, 10
Borden, Joshua, 104–105
Bricker, Darrell, 110
    The Big Shift, 27–28, 31
British Columbia
    pandemic response, 47, 166n30
Brogi, Laura, 80
Brown, Ian, 56–57
Brown, Patrick, 90, 114, 147
    centre-right platform, 61
    connecting with youth, 131
Burke, Edmund, 5, 64, 65
    defence of religious freedom, 91–93
    equality of opportunity, 81
    good order, 110
    social freedom, 73
Butts, Gerald, 28
Byrne, Jenni, 62
    televised debate with Tasha
        Kheiriddin, 62–63

Caesar-Chavannes, Celina, 88
Canada
    allophones as third solitude, 84
    decolonization movement, 84–85
    gratitude for, 85
    nation of immigrants, 12
    national unity issue, 68
    polarization re flag, 86–87
    two founding peoples, 84, 86–87
Canada as global energy superpower
    critical mineral exploration, 143
    increased production of LNG,
        142–43
    national infrastructure corridor, 143
    repealing Bills C-69 and C-48, 142
Canada Child Benefit (Trudeau), 34–36
Canada Recovery Benefit (CRB), 112
Canadian Alliance, 18
Canadian Anti-Hate Network, 55

Canadian Broadcasting Corporation
    (CBC)
    calls for defunding, 17
    Harper's funding cuts to, 23
Canadian Economic Recovery Benefit
    (CERB), 43–44, 112
Canadian flag, disparate meanings
    attached to, 85–86
Canadian Reform Conservative Alliance,
    50
Cardy, Dominic, 72
CBC. *see* Canadian Broadcasting
    Corporation
Centre Ice Conservatives, 72
CERB. *see* Canadian Economic Recovery
    Benefit
Charest, Jean
    Americanization of Canadian
        politics, 69–70
    author's support for, 14
    centre-right platform, 47, 60–61
    connecting with youth, 131
    Convoy Conservatives' view of, 8–9
    family-friendly policies, 94
    national infrastructure corridor, 143
    political orphans, 72
China. *see also* Chinese Communist Party
    Conservative get-tough measures re,
        95–96
    disinformation in 2021 federal
        election, 95–97
    smearing Conservative candidates,
        96–97
Chinese Communist Party (CCP)
    United Front disinformation
        operations, 97
Chiu, Kenny, 96–97
Chong, Michael, 19
Chopra, Tanu, 100, 125, 129
Chrétien, Jean, 67
Cirillo, Corporal Nathan, 25
climate change/environment
    importance to suburban families,
        101

importance to youth, 131
reconciling with resource
    development, 141
reducing emissions, 142
indigenous stewardship, 144
responsible energy development, 145
Clinton, Hillary, 11
Club Conservatives, 14
    characteristics, 8–9
Co-operative Commonwealth Federation
    (CCF), 50
Coalition Avénir Quebec, 148
Common Sense Canadians, 10–11, 13, 73
    winning over, 80
community, youth need for, 130–31
Cong Peiwu, 96
Conservative Party, 148. *See also*
    conservatives in Canada
    addressing populism, 79–82
    adopting family-friendly policies, 94
    anti-debt platform, 2019 election, 39
    beginnings, 50
    beneficiaries of Liberals' misfortunes,
        27–28
    big-tent party, 101
    centre-right political vacuum, filling,
        73
    conspiracy theories rejected by, 58
    credentials requirements issue, 94–95
    embodies conservative principles, 63
    family reunification policies, 93–94
    family values and, 93
    field organizers for community
        outreach, 95
    Freedom Convoy and, 3–4
    freedom of religion and, 91–93
    freedom vs. opportunity as election
        platforms, 74–75
    history of, 15–16
    intolerance/racism image, problem
        with, 58
    lacks diversity, 88
    national security concerns, 95–96
    New Canadian-Old Canada

coalition needed, 31
niqab face-covering issue, 30–31, 91
not assuring New Canadians'
    personal security, 91
pro-Trump leanings, 11–12
recapturing urban/suburban vote,
    106–15
reconciling values and solutions,
    89–92
rights and responsibilities,
    importance of, 69
social cleavages and, 17
suburban residence and support for,
    104–105
Syrian refugee crisis, 30
trending up with youth voters, 124
2015 election campaign, 29–31
youth wing needed, 131
Conservative Party of Quebec, 124
conservatives in Canada. *See also*
    Conservative Party
    building the big tent, 62–70
    different names/brands in history, 16
    federalist-separatist axis and, 66–67
    freedom issues, 63–64
    how they define themselves, 63
    immigration record, 87
    national unity issue, 68
    people vs. elites divide, 8
    populism divides and, 47
    social cleavages in political
        coalitions, 16–17
    society and freedom, 64–65
    traditional issues uniting, 9–10
    widespread discontent among, 7–8
conservatism
    and Canada as impossibilities, 147
    Canadian *vs.* American, 49, 65–66,
        69
    challenged by constantly renewing
        population, 84–85
    equality of opportunity and, 81
    moderating and restraining passions
        (Oakeshott), 68–69

pandemic libertarians, 12
Papillon, Martin, 33
Parsons, Rehtaeh, 21–22
People's Party of Canada (PPC), 38
    anti-debt platform, 2019 election, 39
    anti-immigration position, 88, 56
    far-right elements of, 55
    growth of, 78
    populist threat to Conservative
        Party, 55
Perrella, Andrea M.L., 104–105
Peterson, Jordan, 58, 128
Peterson, Rick, 72
Plamondon, Bob, 15–16, 19
*Plutocrats: The Rise of the New Global
    Super-Rich and the Fall of Everyone
    Else* (Freeland), 38–39
Poilievre, Pierre
    appeal to Quebec voters, 139
    attractive to young voters, 128
    conspiracy theories and, 57–58
    Convoy Conservatives and, 9
    Diefenbaker's influence on, 53–54
    distrust of elites, 51
    emphasizing freedom, 90
    energy policies, 143
    Freedom Convoy and, 3
    freedom quote, 64
    gatekeeper argument, 77
    Indigenous engagement and
        economic reconciliation,
        144–45
    populism of, 47
    root cause of terrorism, 24
    Steam Whistle Brewery rally, 63
    Trump tactics, 56
    use of term Anglo-Saxon, 58
*Political Realignment: A Challenge to
    Thoughtful Canadians* (Ernest and
    Preston Manning), 52–53
populism
    attack the gatekeepers, 108
    blame the elites, 77
    vs. conservativism, 49

economic unfairness and, 76–78
    inequality and, 76
    loss of urban vote and, 108
    social mobility and, 76, 77–78
    wokeism and, 85–87, 114, 126
populism in Canada
    conspiracy theories and, 56–58
    contemporary version of, 56–59
    Diefenbaker and, 53–54
    government debt complaints, 39
    growth of, 38, 78–79, 81
    Harper's populist conservatism,
        48–49
    Justin Trudeau and, 41–43
    leadership issues re, 58–60
    political parties produced by, 49–53
    Preston Manning and, 17
    social-political divides re, 47
    Trudeau's legacy and, 37, 38–47
    using as political end game, 58–59
press, see media
Progressive Conservative Party of Canada
    immigration record, 87
Progressive Party, 49–50, 167n4
Promise and Peril (Wherry), 28
Protzer, Eric, 76–77
    Reclaiming Populism, 77, 78, 81

Quebec
    Bill 21 (niqab face coverings), 61
    Bill 21, conservative leadership
        candidates opposed to, 93
    growth of conservative support in,
        124
    Harper's government and, 19
    pandemic response, 46, 47, 166n30
    parking your vote, 138–39
    separation, battle over, 67, 68
    understanding, 139–40
Québec Solidaire, 148
Quito Maggi, 97

Third solitude, allophones as, 84
Thomas, Jody, 4
Toronto, resentment of, 132–33
Trans Mountain Expansion Project, 34
trucker protest, Ottawa, *see* Freedom
  Convoy
Trudeau, Justin, 11
  anti-abortion groups excluded from
    summer jobs program, 42–43
  blackface, 41, 42
  Boston Marathon terrorism remarks,
    24
  Canada Child Benefit, 34–36,
    163n33
  cannabis legalization, 34
  carbon tax, 34
  effort-result disconnect and, 36–37
  elected leader of Liberal Party, 27,
    28–29
  electoral reform failure, 32–33
  enrages Western Canada, 43
  father's eulogy, 28
  Freedom Convoy and, 1–3, 5
  gender equality issues, 43
  government, growth of, 33, 36, 37,
    38–39
  and growth of populism, 37, 38–47,
    78
  housing affordability, 46
  hypocrisy on social justice issues,
    41–43
  identity politics, 39–40, 41
  inexperience of, 29
  as Laurentian Elite incarnate, 28
  middle-class salaries decline under,
    35–36, 163n35
  no reconciliation with Indigenous
    Peoples, 33–34
  opposite of Harper, 29
  overpromising, 31–32, 161n18
  overspending, 32, 162n21
  Sabrevois town hall, 42
  2015 election campaign, 29–31
Trudeau, Pierre Elliot, 2, 90

multiculturalism and, 84, 141
Trump, Donald
  identity politics and, 40
  Maxime Bernier compared to, 55
  populist-based support, 48
  professed sympathy for the excluded,
    11
  support for Freedom Convoy, 1
two solitudes, Canada, 66

United Conservative Party of Alberta, 52
United Front, CCP disinformation
  operations, 97
United States
  conservativism different from
    Canadian, 65–66, 69
  Freedom Caucus, 10
  freedom, concept of, 65
  identity politics and Trump election,
    40
  opportunity conservativism, 75–76
urban vote, 99–115
  abortion policy, 109–10
  Conservative erosion in, 103–6
  conservative representation in
    municipal government, 112–14
  energy policy, 111–12
  gun control, 111
  housing affordability and, 106–109
  immigration, urbanization and
    Liberal vote, 105–106
  local issues and, 111
  losing, 102
  millennials, 122
  municipal voter turnout, 113
  new class and, 104
  905 corridor, 101
  pandemic policies, 112
  public safety, 110–11
  recapturing, 106–15
  rural-urban divide, 102–103
  school boards, 114
  seat redistribution, 105